Ashton Oxenden

The pathway of Safety, or, Counsel to the Awakened

Ashton Oxenden

The pathway of Safety, or, Counsel to the Awakened

ISBN/EAN: 9783743341548

Manufactured in Europe, USA, Canada, Australia, Japa

Cover: Foto ©ninafisch / pixelio.de

Manufactured and distributed by brebook publishing software (www.brebook.com)

Ashton Oxenden

The pathway of Safety, or, Counsel to the Awakened

THE PATHWAY OF SAFETY;

OR,

COUNSEL TO THE AWAKENED.

BY THE
REV. ASHTON OXENDEN,
RECTOR OF PLUCKLEY, KENT,
AND HON. CANON OF CANTERBURY.

One Hundred and Sixty-fourth Thousand.

LONDON:
WILLIAM MACINTOSH,
24, PATERNOSTER-ROW.
1869.

CONTENTS.

	Page
THE OBJECT OF THE BOOK . .	vii

CHAPTER I.

WHAT IT IS TO BE AWAKENED . . 1

CHAPTER II.

SALVATION—HOW IT IS OBTAINED . 12

CHAPTER III.

HELPS BY THE WAY.

The Lord's-day. — God's House. — Public Prayer.—Hearing God's Word.—The Holy Communion 20

CHAPTER IV.

HELPS BY THE WAY.

Private Prayer and Praise 44

CHAPTER V.

HELPS BY THE WAY.

The Bible 65

CHAPTER VI.

HELPS BY THE WAY.

Religious Books.—Religious Intercourse.—Meditation.—Communion with God.—Self-examination 78

CHAPTER VII.

CHURCH MEMBERSHIP . . 97

CHAPTER VIII.

DANGERS FROM WITHOUT.

The World.—Loose and Ungodly Friendships.—Persecution . . . 110

CHAPTER IX.

DANGERS FROM WITHIN.

An Evil Heart.—Pride.—Temper.—Uncharitableness.—Selfishness.—Idleness.—Influence of Bad Habits 130

CHAPTER X.

TEMPTATIONS OF SATAN. . . . 156

CHAPTER XI.

DIFFICULTIES.

Weakness of Faith.—A Sense of Sinfulness.—Wanderings in Prayer.—The Duty of Confessing Christ.—Perplexing Passages of Scripture 175

CHAPTER XII.

CAUTIONS.

True and False Repentance.—An Unstable Course.—Religious Excitement.—False Teaching 196

CHAPTER XIII.

DUTIES.

To God.—To One's Family.—To One's Fellow-Christians.—To the Worldly.—To the Heathen.—To Oneself 212

CHAPTER XIV.

Encouragements . . 232

CHAPTER XV.

Progress and Relapse . . 244

CHAPTER XVI.

The Discipline of Affliction . 256

CHAPTER XVII.

Usefulness . . 266

CHAPTER XVIII.

Happiness . . . 282

THE OBJECT OF THE BOOK.

I WRITE this book specially for one class of persons—not a very large class I fear, but certainly a very important class. These pages contain some christian counsel for those, who, through God's mercy, have been awakened out of their spiritual sleep, and who now feel that there is a great journey before them, and a happy land which they are most anxious one day to reach. And, if I mistake not, these are the very persons who are ready to receive, with a hearty welcome, a little advice from one who is desirous to lead them right.

Are you, my dear reader, one of this class? Are you beginning to feel concerned about your soul? Is that earnest cry which came from the Philippian Jailor's heart just the very language of your's—" What must I do to be saved?" If so, happy are you. It is the Lord's doing. Nothing less than his Almighty power has aroused you; and that same power must keep you to the end. The salvation of a soul is God's work from first to last. But He is pleased to employ ministers, and books, and various other instruments, to carry on his work in the soul, and to bring it at last to heaven.

Now if I know anything of the secret history of *your* soul, I think I am not wrong in saying that many a doubt and many a difficulty oftentimes comes across you. A few words then of counsel and guidance will not be out of place. Perhaps you will say, "This is just what I want. If any one will only take me by the hand, and lead me through my difficulties, such help will indeed be most seasonable; and it will be of no small service to me in the present state of my soul. Only show me the *Pathway of Safety*, and I will endeavour, by God's help, to walk in it."

May the Holy Spirit be both your Director and mine, guiding *me* as to what I shall say, and preparing *your* heart to profit by my words.

THE PATHWAY OF SAFETY.

CHAPTER I.

WHAT IT IS TO BE AWAKENED.

We all know what *natural* Sleep is. The body has for a time lost its power. It is, to all appearance, dead and motionless. The eyes see not; the tongue speaks not; the hands and feet move not. Its state is like that of a watch when it is not wound up.

We all know, too, what it is to be aroused from such a sleep. We are brought back to life, as it were. We have fresh powers given to us. Our sight is restored, and all our lost energies return.

Now, there is such a thing as *spiritual* Sleep, —the sleep of *the soul*. Alas! many souls are thus asleep. Is it not so? Else how is it, that when we are told of "a wrath to come," so few are taking any steps to escape it? How is it, that, when heaven is offered to us, so few are seeking it?—that although Christ has shed His blood, so few are caring for it? Ah! it is too true that men are *asleep*, as regards their *souls* and *eternity*.

If we want to know *how* it is that this sleep has come upon us, we have only to look at Gen. iii.; or Rom. v. We there learn, that when sin had once made its entrance into the world, man became a fallen creature; his soul, from that moment, was stunned as it were; a deadly slumber crept over it. And hence it is that we see men all alive as to worldly things, but all asleep, and even dead, as to spiritual things.

And was it not once so with *you?* Perhaps you may have lived ten, twenty, or even forty years, without any real concern about your salvation, or about the world to which you were hastening. In your earliest days you were solemnly brought to Christ; you were given to Him in baptism; you were numbered among His sheep; you were marked as one of His; the Good Shepherd received you into the arms of His mercy. But, oh, how soon you forsook Him! You still bore His honoured name. You still called yourself a Christian, and others called you so too; but that was all. It might be said of you, as it was of the Christians at Sardis, " Thou hast a name that thou livest, and art *dead*."

Think what your state was at that time. You heard of heaven; but you thought little about it. You heard of hell; but it seemed like an idle tale that you had no need to attend to. You heard of a Saviour; but His love did not reach your heart. You believed Him perhaps to be the Saviour of *the world:* but you never applied to Him to save *you*. He seemed only as a stranger afar off; and you cared not to draw near to Him. You heard of eternity; but the passing things of time were all that you troubled yourself about. You made preparation for days and years to come in this world; but no preparation was made for that world which is eternal. You were keen eyed and zealous enough about the things of earth; you followed with much eagerness its recreations and employments; but those things which concerned your soul were either altogether neglected, or done slowly and heavily; and your spirit moved like Pharaoh's chariot when the wheels were off. You read God's word occasionally, perhaps daily; but it was a dull book to you : it did not interest you; it only reached the surface. You repeated, day by day, words of prayer; but you never *prayed*. There was no *heart*-work with you. You listened to sermons; but the gospel passed over your mind, just as the bright sunbeam glides over the closed window without ever entering in. There was light all around you—a blessed light from above—but your heart was closed, and not one ray reached it.

And what must we say of you all this while, but that your soul was asleep—fast asleep; not *dozing* merely, but buried in a deep, sound slumber? There was no feeling, and no life in it.

But perhaps *now*, through God's grace, your state is altogether changed. You see things clearly which, a few months, or a few years, back, you did not see at all. You are now *awakened*. You feel an anxiety, which you never felt before. Your one chief inquiry is, how you may obtain pardon, and how salvation may become yours—how you may be forgiven and accepted of God now, and how you can be admitted into the blessed company of His saints hereafter. You are much in the same state as the Prodigal, when he "*came to himself,*" and said, "I will arise, and go to my father, and say unto him, Father, I have sinned against heaven, and before thee, and am no more worthy to be called thy son." (Luke xv. 17—19.) It is with you as it was with Lydia, when "the Lord opened her heart." (Acts xvi. 14.) As great a change has taken place in you as in St. Paul, who, from being a blind persecutor of Christ, became one of his most zealous and devoted followers. From *your* eyes, as well as his, the "scales" have fallen; and "whereas you *were* blind, *now* you see." (Acts ix. 18; John ix. 25.) It is true, you do not yet see *all*, for there is some darkness remaining in you; but still you see much that you never saw before.

And do you not yourself feel like a man awakened out of sleep? Do you not seem to be almost in a new world? Do you not feel those words to be most true in your case, "If any man be in Christ, he is *a new creature: old things are passed away: behold, all things are become new*"? (2 Cor. v. 17.) A *new life* seems to open before you; you have *new feelings* within you; *new objects* to live for; *new hopes* to cheer you; and you have entered upon the service of a *new Master*.

Think, my dear friend, how great has been God's love to you, how great is the forbearance He has shown you, and the patience with which He waited for your return to Him. He saw you careless and rebellious, and when He called you, you refused; but still He spared you. Again and again you resisted the Holy Spirit; and yet that Spirit strove with you, till at length He won you over to himself. Oh, what exceeding love was this! Who can tell the length, and breadth, and height, and depth of it? And this God, whom you have slighted, and disobeyed, and trifled with—this God is still ready to bless you, and to make you happy!

And now you wish, I think, to serve Him— do you not? You can now see that an earnest religious life is the only life that can give you peace. And it is your heart's desire to live such a life. You almost envy those who are true Christians, and you wish to be one of them. In short, your present purpose is to cast in your lot with the people of God.

Here, however, let me throw in a word or

two of caution—not to discourage you, but because it is very needful that you should be sure of your ground as you go on.

There is such a thing as *an awakening of the feelings,* without any *awakening of the heart.* I have known persons touched by a sermon, for instance, so that their tears have flowed, and they appeared to be spiritually aroused. Their affections have been so moved that they have fancied at the time that they could give up all for Christ. For the moment they seemed to be roused, and desirous of living a new life. And yet all quickly passed away, "as the morning cloud, and as the early dew." There was no inward work of the Spirit upon the heart. The soul was in fact still asleep. It was disturbed a little, but *never fairly awakened.*

Examine yourself, then, closely, and see whether *a real inward change* is taking place, and whether the Holy Spirit is now at work, within you. And if it be so, let me tell you what will be your feelings. You will not only be ready to acknowledge your sin, but you will feel bitter *sorrow* for it. The thought of having sinned against God will make you unhappy. You would give worlds to recall the past. It grieves you now to think of hours and days that you have wasted; of Sabbaths misspent; of a neglected Bible; of many an idle word that you have spoken; of many a hard saying that escaped your lips; and of the evil temper, which perhaps you tried so little to curb. The thought that you have lived so much to the world and to self, instead of living to Christ—that you had a gracious and loving Saviour, though you knew Him not—that you have again and again grieved the Holy Spirit by the hardness and coldness of your heart—all this, and much more, rushes into your mind, and pierces you to the very quick. All the ten thousand sins, in short, that you committed, or had *the will to commit*, though you lacked the opportunity, now come up before you. The recollection of these painful facts fills you with the keenest sorrow. You feel that you can get no rest, until you find it in Christ; and the one great desire of your heart is to live a life of holiness and devotedness to His service.

But I have another word of caution for you. Some may try to persuade you that you are not truly converted, unless you can give a clear account of *all the particulars* of your awakening. But this is altogether a mistake. It is not necessary to be able to say *how, when,* or *where*, you were first religiously impressed. "The wind bloweth where it listeth, and thou hearest the sound thereof, but canst not tell whence it cometh, and whither it goeth; so is every one that is born of the Spirit." (John iii. 8.) As to the precise *manner* in which you were awakened, it matters little. The great question is whether God has by any means savingly aroused your soul; and if so, you cannot be sufficiently thankful.

Neither, again, is it necessary that the experience of *all Christians* should be *precisely alike;* indeed, facts show that it is not so. God leads some in one way, and some in another. Because one Christian may have gone through this or that particular stage of feeling, it does not follow that *you* should have felt just the same. We are not all brought to God by the same means; neither does the self-same process go on in every heart. Some are not led to believe in Christ, and to love Him, without passing through severe trials and painful conflicts. They are snatched as " brands from the burning; " they are " saved with fear," " pulled out of the fire." In other souls the work of grace has proceeded unobserved by those around, and even perhaps almost unknown to the individuals themselves. Their hearts are naturally docile, and are as easily moulded as water is to the shape of the bottle into which it is poured. Of course I do not mean that they are *born* Christians; but they become so by such a gentle and gradual change, that they miss much of that severe conflict which others pass through. After all, it matters little *how* we were first brought to God: the great question is, *have* we been savingly brought to Him? Are we grieved for our past sins? Do we long for holiness of heart? Are we cleaving to Christ, and serving Him?

Now, before we go any further together, let me ask you to pause for a few minutes, and put up a short prayer to God. Perhaps the following may help you:—

A THANKFUL PRAYER FOR ONE WHO IS AWAKENED.

O Almighty Father, I confess to Thee how utterly worthless my past life has been. I have sinned against heaven, and before Thee, and am no more worthy to be called Thy child. But, in Thy great mercy, Thou hast brought me out of this my ruined state. Thou hast given sight to my blind eyes, and awakened my slumbering soul. O my God, I heartily thank Thee for this. Blot out, I beseech Thee, for Jesus Christ's sake, all my sins, known and unknown, past and present; and make me henceforth to be Thy true servant.

Blessed Lord, work in me a real inward change. Do Thou begin it, if it is not already begun, and carry it on, if it is. May it be indeed *Thy* work. Oh! let me not deceive myself in so great a matter. May thy blessed Spirit enlighten me, teach me, and comfort me. Leave me not, neither forsake me, O God of my salvation. Enable me from this hour to give myself, heart and soul, to Thee. I desire to devote myself to Thy service, and to be all that Thou wouldest have me to be.

Give me faith, that I may believe in Christ, and live closer and closer to Him day by day. Give me courage, that I may make a bold stand for Christ. Give me strength, that I may resist temptation. Give me meekness and lowliness of heart, that I may walk humbly with my God. Make me thine now, and thine for ever. Grant this, I beseech Thee, for Jesus Christ's sake. *Amen.*

CHAPTER II.

SALVATION—HOW IT IS OBTAINED.

THIS is a subject of the deepest importance to every anxious soul. I trust that it is to yours. Once, the chief questions you seemed inclined to ask were, " What shall I eat ? " or, " How shall I dress ? " or, " Where can I find pleasure ? " or, " How can I get rich ? " But all these questions have now given place to one far more pressing—" I am concerned about my soul: how can I find salvation for it ? What must I do to be saved ? "

I have often thought that the most pitiable state for a man to be in must be this—when he feels his sinfulness and his danger, and is conscious of having offended God ; but yet has no means of knowing where he may find mercy, no friend to point out to him any one bright spot, whither he may turn his anxious eyes in the hope of obtaining peace. I believe that among the heathen such cases often occur. There is many a man, who has for years felt sin to be a heavy burden, and has longed for relief. He has earnestly sought for peace, but in vain : he has never found it. He has tried this and that remedy, but all to no purpose; for, alas, he is ignorant of the only true remedy, and he has no one to bring it to him. He is like a weary wayworn traveller, passing through some desert land, who longs to quench his burning thirst, but there is no one to point out to him the refreshing stream, which he so eagerly desires. It may be all the while within his reach, but he knows it not; and thus his thirst remains unsatisfied. And may there not be many in heathen lands who are thus weary and thirsty, and have no one to point Him out to them who says, "Come unto me, all ye that labour and are heavy laden, and I will give you rest"?

But, thank God, it cannot be so with *you*. You have God's Word, and God's Ministers; and from them you may get the direction which you so greatly need. And what do they tell you?

They tell you, first of all, that **you** cannot

save yourself. No; this is utterly out of your power. For what is your condition? You have sinned, and forfeited heaven; you are in debt with God; you have lost His favour; and if you had your strict desert, it would be eternal death: for is it not written, "The wages of sin is death;" and again, "The soul that sinneth, it shall die"? Ezek. xviii. 4; Rom. vi. 23.

No; you cannot recover yourself. You are utterly unable to atone for your sins. You cannot win back the heaven which you have lost. You cannot undo the evil which you have done. If from this moment you could live a perfectly holy and spotless life, you could not put away even one of the least of your past sins. It would be as if a man were to run in debt, and then were to go to his creditors and say, "I am grieved that I should have treated you so wrongly. I implore you not to press me for the sum that is due. I am resolved from this time to incur no *fresh* debt." Now, would this satisfy the creditors, and clear off *what is already owing?* Certainly not; for the debt would still remain unsettled, unless some one kindly came forward to pay it. Just so is it with *your* sins. You are a debtor to

God; and not one item of the heavy debt are you able to pay off *yourself*.

How, then, you will ask, can this be done? How can we obtain salvation for our souls which so much need it? How can we escape the hell we so richly deserve? How can we obtain favour with the God whom we have offended? How can we ever reach heaven? These are stirring questions for an awakened sinner to ask; and they shall not go unanswered. From no quarter but one can salvation be obtained; no power but one can reach the hidden seat of our disease: no hand but one can touch the sufferer, and set him free from the cruel bondage under which he groans. Blessed be God, although *we* have no remedy in our own hands, *He* has provided one for us. He has looked upon us in our lost state, and has sent His Son to redeem us. That dear Saviour has shed His blood upon the cross, and has thereby made a full, perfect, and sufficient sacrifice for sin. He died, "the just for the unjust, that he might bring us to God." (1 Pet. iii. 18.) He "bare our sins in his own body on the tree." 1 Pet. ii. 24.

Here is salvation for the guiltiest. We tell you to pray; we bid you go and weep for your sins; we exhort you to lead a new life. But we tell you also that neither your *prayers*, be they ever so earnest; nor your *contrition*, be it ever so deep; nor your *new life*, however complete the change, can purchase your acceptance with God, or even put away one single sin. Only the blood of Jesus Christ can do this. He has power to save, and He alone. He has paid the debt, which you yourself could never pay.

Still you will ask, " How can I be saved? There is salvation for us, I know; but how can I make this salvation *mine?* " Suppose you lost your way on some dark night, and fell into a deep pit, so deep that you had not power to escape from it; and whilst you lay there, in a state of utter helplessness, some kind person were to come and have pity on you, and let down a rope to rescue you,—what would you do? Would you not stretch out your hand, and seize the rope? Would you not lay hold of it with thankfulness? So is it with Christ and the sinner. We must stretch out the hand of faith; and so lay hold of the salvation offered, and make it *ours*. " By Grace," says the Apostle, " are ye saved through faith." (Eph. ii. 8.) *Grace* is, as it were, the rope held out to the drowning man; and *Faith* is the hand that seizes it, and lays hold of it. Happy those who have experienced this deliverance! They can say with the Psalmist, " He brought me up out of an horrible pit, out of the miry clay, and set my feet upon a rock, and established my goings." (Ps. xl. 2.)

A direct application, then, must be made to Christ to save you. Look steadily to Him for pardon, peace, life, and salvation. As the poor perishing Israelite looked eagerly towards the brazen serpent and was healed (Num. xxi. 9; John iii. 14, 15), so do you look with the eye of faith to Jesus; and in Him you shall surely find fulness of pardon and peace here, and a life that will last for ever.

When I say that we must come to Christ in faith, I mean this—He is in heaven, and we are on earth. We cannot *see* Him, and yet He is near to us, and ready (oh, how ready!) to help us. All we can do then is to ask Him, to beg Him, to entreat Him, to receive us. All we can do is to throw ourselves, as it were, at His feet, and surrender ourselves to Him. This is faith. It is believing that Christ can save us; it is putting ourselves into His hands.

But many an awakened Christian is sometimes kept back by this thought,—"Will Christ save such an one as I am? He will receive those who come to Him with true repentance, and strong faith; but I fear that I have *neither*. My heart is too hard to repent, and my faith is sadly mixed with unbelief. Surely I must wait till I am holier and better, before He will deign to look upon me." No, no; Jesus came to save *the lost;* and are not *you* lost? He came like a Physician, to heal *the sick*, and not *the whole*. If you were famishing, would you refuse a rich repast provided for you, *because you were so hungry?* If you were perishing of cold, would you shrink from the fire, because you were shivering and comfortless?

Though your faith is very weak—only as a little grain of mustard seed—be encouraged. Jesus will strengthen it. He will not turn away from you. You are welcome to Him. And though you feel yourself sadly weak and unworthy, yet the arms of His mercy are open to receive you.

Wait not then a single moment; but come just as you are to the loving Saviour. Lay all your sins at the foot of the cross, with this only plea upon your lips—that you are a poor needy sinner, and that He is an Almighty Saviour.

Remember, then, this great truth—this foundation truth of Scripture—this truth which is written, as it were, with a sunbeam on the pages of God's word—that SALVATION IS IN CHRIST, AND IN CHRIST ALONE. He is your Remedy, your Ransom, your Sacrifice, your Hope, your All. " Behold the Lamb of God, which taketh away the sin of the world." " Believe on the Lord Jesus Christ, and thou shalt be saved." John i. 29; Acts xvi. 31.

> " He *nothing* knows, who knows not this,
> That earth can yield no settled bliss,
>   No lasting portion give.
> He *all things* knows, who knows to place
> His hopes on Christ's redeeming grace,
>   Who died that we might live."

CHAPTER III.

HELPS BY THE WAY.

THE LORD'S DAY.—GOD'S HOUSE.—PUBLIC PRAYER.—SERMONS.—THE HOLY COMMUNION.

Christ alone saves us. I have dwelt awhile upon this in the last chapter, because I feel that this truth is the groundwork, the foundation-stone, the rock on which we must build. And I feel it to be of the very utmost importance to *you*, dear reader—to you who are already awakened, and concerned about your soul—to have this vital point clearly and strongly fixed in your mind. Jesus it is who, from first to last, must save you; and, as you pursue your onward course, you must, day by day, be looking unto Him.

But now, let me point out to you some of those gracious Helps, which He affords us by the way. I shall speak, in this Chapter, of the *Outward Helps;* or, as they are usually called, the *Public Means of Grace.*

I. THE LORD'S-DAY.

This is the Christian's day; a day given to him by God, to have his body rested, his mind refreshed, his soul prospered—a hallowed and a happy day. Learn to prize it as one of your greatest blessings. You think of God, and draw near to Him, I trust, *every* day in the week. But *this* is the special day, on which the Great King seems to hold his court, and his people are pressingly invited to come into His presence. On other days blessings descend upon our souls like *dew;* but on this day the Lord opens, as it were, the very windows of heaven, and *showers* these blessings down upon us in large measure. You will find that "the great secret of a happy week is a holy Sabbath." Give that day entirely to God, and you will have the less difficulty in walking with Him during other days.

On Saturday evening let all your week-day work be finished. And then ask God to prepare your heart for the morrow. When you awake in the morning, say to yourself, "This is the day the Lord hath made, I will rejoice and be glad in it." It is a good thing to begin the day by getting your heart tuned for the holy employments which are before you. Entreat a blessing on all the services, in which you are about to engage. And forget not to ask God to be with your Minister, and to enable him " rightly to divide the word of truth," so that he may give to each one the allotted portion as he needs it.

Let your Sundays be *holy* days ; and let them also be *cheerful and happy* days—precious seasons of refreshment, to help you forward on your way. Some there are who hang down their heads, and put on a mournful look, on the Lord's day; but this is wrong. For the sake of others, we should shew that " the Sabbath " is " our delight ; " and for our own sakes, too, we should regard it as a sweet foretaste of that joyous Sabbath, which we shall for ever spend in God's house above.

Do you love your Sundays? You did not love them once. They were a weariness to you. You were glad when they were over. But now, I trust, you look upon them as so many bright and sunny spots in the journey of life. Be much with God on this day. Converse with Him, as with a Father ; and learn from the Holy Spirit those great lessons, which none but He can teach you. And just as, on some warm day in summer, the grass grows apace, and the fruit ripens in a few hours more than for days and weeks before, so may each Sunday be to you a day of much spiritual growth, a blessed ripening for heaven!

> O sweetest day of all the seven,
> Emblem and earnest of that heaven
>   Where saints have peace and rest ;
> For thee I thirst, for thee I sigh,
> And count the hours till thou art nigh,
>   Sweet day of sacred rest.
>
> O let my heart thus sigh and glow,
> My song no intermission know,
>   Till death shall seal my tongue ;
> In heaven a holier strain I'll raise,
> And rest from everything but praise—
>   My heaven one endless song.
>
> H. Smith.

II. GOD'S HOUSE.

There was a time when you went to church as a matter of form, or for decency's sake, or to satisfy conscience; but now you go for quite another reason—because you delight in being there. Your happiest moments are spent within those sacred walls; and you feel it good to join your fellow-Christians at the hour of prayer. David's words now find an echo in your heart; "I was glad when they said unto me, Let us go into the house of the Lord;" "A day in thy courts is better than a thousand." Psalm lxxxiv. 10; cxxii. 1.

The moment you enter God's house, try and get a feeling of *reverence* upon your mind. The Lord says, "Reverence my sanctuary." (Lev. xxvi. 2.) And surely it is no light thing to be in His presence. You remember what He said to Moses, when he drew near to the burning bush; and that bush was for the time a sacred place, for God was there:—"Put off thy shoes from off thy feet; for the place whereon thou standest is holy ground." (Ex. iii. 5.) Always keep this idea strongly fixed in your mind—that God's house is a *holy* place. It is His temple, the presence-chamber of the great King, where He promises to be in the midst of His servants. Let your feeling be something like Jacob's at Bethel, when he exclaimed, "Surely the Lord is in this place. This is none other but the house of God, and this is the gate of heaven." Gen. xxviii. 17.

It is most important to accustom our minds to a feeling of solemn awe, the moment we enter God's courts. This will do a great deal towards keeping us from wandering and trifling thoughts, and will help us to realize His presence.

Remember that the hours you spend there are most precious hours, for which you will have to give a strict reckoning. Prize them, then, and make much of them, for they will soon pass away. You can read at home, it is true, and you can pray in secret; but is it nothing to be told by your Lord, " Where two or three are gathered together in my name, *there am I in the midst* of them"? (Matt. xviii. 20.)

But you are in danger in God's sanctuary, as well as elsewhere. Satan will endeavour to draw away your eyes, and make them wander, and to steal away your heart, and fix it on some trifling object. Wherever seed is cast in a field, the birds of the air follow, ready to devour the grain. And where the seed of God's word is sown, there will " the wicked one" be on the watch to " snatch it away." Ask God, then, to fix his truth in your heart, and to cause it to root there by the power of his Holy Spirit. Ask Him to keep you by his grace, or you may go to the house of God Sunday after Sunday and yet miss the blessings which He is so ready to give you. Make this a special subject of care and watchfulness.

III. PUBLIC PRAYER.

This is one great object for which we go to the house of the Lord—to unite in prayer with our Christian brethren, and to kneel with them as one family before God. The Lord himself has given his house a name—" My house shall be called a house of *Prayer*." (Matt. xxi. 13.) Look upon it in this light—not merely as a place of *Hearing,* or a place of *Preaching,* but as a House of *Prayer.*

Many go there merely to sit and listen. And if they remain quiet and attentive whilst the prayers are offered up, they think there is not much amiss. But *you* know the value of prayer. Go, then, for this special object—to *pray.* Join in the prayers, not only outwardly with your voice, but inwardly with your heart. Make it a time of earnest supplication. "Draw nigh to God, and He will draw nigh to you."

I need hardly urge upon you here the duty of *kneeling* in the house of God: for I cannot imagine any really earnest Christian using any other posture in the Lord's presence.

As a member of the Church of England, be

thankful that we have a regular Form of Public Prayer; be thankful that we can use the very words which God's people have used for hundreds of years before us, and which thousands both in our own land and in far-off countries are using at the same time with ourselves. There is something very delightful in the thought, that other hearts are finding utterance in the very same expressions which we ourselves are pouring forth to our Father in heaven; and that those who are most dear to us are approaching Him with the same petitions as ourselves. There is too a calm, peaceful, and devout earnestness about our Church prayers, which grows upon us the more heartily we use them.

You may sometimes meet with those who dislike *Forms of prayer*, and they will perhaps taunt you by saying that our Church prayers are *dead men's prayers*. But no, it will be far otherwise, if we have only earnest hearts to use them. They will be *living* prayers, if only the life of God is in our souls. Those holy men and martyrs who framed them, it is true, have long since passed away from this world; but could they have left us a more precious legacy for our use than this "form of sound words?"

These very men, we believe, are now " before the throne of God," having exchanged the voice of prayer for that of endless praise.

Prize, then, your Church prayers; and enter into the spirit of them. We may use a Form of prayer without being *formal,* if the Spirit of God does but touch our hearts, and open our lips. And if you find an increased enjoyment in this part of the service, I know of scarcely any surer proof that your soul is in a healthy state; for it shows that prayer is a comfort to you, not because you are excited for the moment, but because you feel a steady, fixed, desire to wait upon God, and to make known your requests unto Him. It is easy enough to be warmed up for the time by a fervent extempore prayer, which "seems to go through one," as the saying is. But, alas! how soon our devotion, when thus worked up, dies down again; and then it leaves the heart cold and languid!

But do not mistake me. I would on no account throw a slight on extempore prayer. There are times when the awakened heart will, and must, speak for itself; for no words but its own can express all it feels. But I would guard you against the notion that extempore prayer is more suitable for *Public* Worship, and more profitable for a Congregation, than a Liturgy like our own.

I cannot leave this subject without saying a word or two about *wandering thoughts*. Perhaps you are ready to complain that these trouble you. Yes, it may be you have often grieved, when the closing prayer is offered that you have prayed so little. Who has not felt this? Let us carefully watch against it, and entreat God to keep us from thus dishonouring Him. Steadily and earnestly set yourself to correct this habit of inattention; and you will find, by degrees, that the temptation will grow weaker, and prayer become more and more delightful to you. You will find, too, that the more enjoyment you have in public prayer, the more your soul will grow and prosper.

IV. HEARING GOD'S WORD.

Great things are stated in the Bible with regard to Preaching. It is said to *save* us; " Receive with meekness the engrafted word, which is able to *save* your souls." (James i. 21.) " It pleased God, by the foolishness of preaching, to *save* them that believe." (1 Cor. i. 21.)

We can hardly value too highly the preaching of the Gospel as a Christian ordinance. Three thousand souls were converted by it on the Day of Pentecost. It is by this instrument that God is often pleased to arouse the sinner, and to strengthen and build up his own people.

Have you never gone to church cold and dull, and something from the preacher's lips has fallen like a beam of light upon your heart, and has sent you home rejoicing? We may liken it to the effect we have sometimes seen on a summer's morning, when the sun mounts above the horizon; but the whole landscape beneath is bathed in mist. Suddenly a gleam bursts through it; the gloom is dispersed, and all is clear and bright. And has it not at times been so with *you?* Some word spoken in God's house has come as a message of light to your soul, and you have gone home relieved and gladdened: every mist has been cleared away.

Listen *with deep attention* to every sermon you hear; for it concerns the very life of your soul. Do not hear for others: hear for yourself. Listen *with faith,* believing that the Lord himself speaks to you by His ambassador. Listen *with prayerfulness,* continually lifting up your heart to God; for what you need is

His blessing on the seed sown; and remember, there is one by your side ready to snatch it away. Listen *with humility and teachableness;* for whilst here you will never be able to say, I have nothing more to learn. I feel that one of the faults of the present day is a lack of this humility. The direction of the Apostle is forgotten, "Receive with *meekness* the engrafted word." And it is on this account that the word preached does not profit us so much as it might. Cultivate a spirit of humility, and seek to have the mind of Mary, who was content to sit at the feet of Jesus, and hear His word.

Endeavour to *carry away* as much as you can of every sermon. Think it over when you get home, and lay it up in the storehouse of your heart. The seed, unless it is worked in below the surface of the soil, will never spring up and bear fruit. It is " the *entrance* " of God's word that " giveth light." Ps. cxix. 130.

Are we careful and watchful enough over ourselves on *leaving* the house of God? When the sermon is ended, and the service is over, let us not think that the work is done. We must then be cautious lest we lose the store which we have gathered, lest the fire which has been lighted within us be quenched, lest the seed which has been sown should rot upon the surface. Avoid, as much as possible, worldly and trifling conversation on your way home. And, as soon as you are able, it may be well to retire to your chamber for a few minutes of secret prayer to God, asking Him to bless what you have heard, and fix it in your heart. And during the week you should be constantly calling to mind, and carrying out in your daily life, the truths and precepts which have been set before you.

Our Lord once said to his disciples, " Take heed how ye hear." And we have great reason to *take heed*, lest the Tempter rob us of the offered blessing. Pray *before* you hear—*whilst* you are hearing—and *after* you have heard. *Before*, that God would prepare your heart; *whilst* hearing, that God would bring home his word to your very soul; and *after*, that the precious seed may take root, and bear fruit an hundredfold.

Sometimes it happens that we are tempted to find fault with the Preacher. His voice is too low or too loud; his manner does not please us; or his language is not to our taste. We are on the look out for defects, and are far too apt to fasten on any little fault in the minister, and make it an excuse for our inattention. Resist this by every means; and rather be disposed to find fault with *yourself*. Again, it seems to gratify our natural pride and vanity to be able to pull a sermon to pieces, and shew how this difficulty might have been better explained, and that doctrine more clearly stated. We find others around us perhaps doing this, and we think that they must needs have much spiritual grace and discernment. But I hardly know of a more dangerous practice to indulge in, and I would earnestly guard you against it. I believe it to be one of Satan's great devices for robbing us of that which would otherwise nourish our souls. He likes thus to busy us with the outside shell, whilst he carefully draws away the precious kernel. The ministry of the Gospel has been committed to " earthen vessels, that the excellency of the power may be of *God*," and not of *man*. The vessel may be plain; but God's blessing may be with it. The hand that sows the seed may be feeble; but He can " give the increase." The words of the minister may be poor in themselves, or his matter dry, or his manner of delivering his message unwelcome;

but there is something to be gleaned from every sermon—there is something in it that may do you good. Listen, then, not *to find fault*, but *to be fed;* and thus you will get many a refreshing meal, whilst others are sent empty away. Look not so much to the hand that brings the food to you, or at the manner in which it is dealt out to you; but look to the food itself, and try to gather from it all the nourishment you can. Look above the messenger, to Him who sends you the message. Let the humble, teachable spirit of Cornelius be yours, " Now, therefore, we are all here present before God, to hear all things that are commanded thee of God." Acts x. 33.

Again, take it as a bad sign, when you begin to get restless and discontented, and when you are constantly desiring to hear strange preachers. This is often the case with newly awakened persons. They are inclined to think that they cannot hear too much. Thus their minds get into a feverish state; they are "tossed about with every wind of doctrine," and they are for ever hungering after some change of spiritual food. I would affectionately warn you against this. It is a bad and unhealthy state to get into. There are some spoken of in Scripture, who are " ever learning, and never able to come to the knowledge of the truth." (2 Tim. iii. 7.) They go here and there with open ears, but lay up no food and nourishment in their souls. We are told, too, of others, who " spent their time in nothing else, but either to tell or to hear some new thing." (Acts xvii. 21.) Beware of this unstable and unsettled state of mind. Value the preaching of God's word highly—as highly as you please. But let it be for the truth's sake, and not to satisfy an itching ear, or a restless fancy. God has placed you under a settled ministry: remain faithful to it. If you once get into a wandering and restless spirit, you will be nearly sure to suffer loss. Stay where you are; and earnestly entreat God himself to feed and fill your soul.

And here let me put in a further word of advice. Besides receiving thankfully the truths which your Minister proclaims to you in public, you should look upon him as your *Counsellor* in all spiritual matters. It is written, " The priest's lips should keep knowledge, and they should seek the law at his mouth, for he is the messenger of the Lord of hosts." (Mal. ii. 7.) Then go to him in all your difficulties. Fly to him for advice. Open your heart to him. Tell him of all that perplexes you. Many things, which he has set before you from the pulpit, he may be able to unfold to you more fully in private. And if there should be anything either in God's word, or in God's dealings with you, which causes you some little anxiety, he may be able to throw such further light upon it, as may greatly relieve your mind. Regard him, in short, as the Messenger of God to *you*, and as the spiritual Physician who can administer healing medicines to *your* soul.

V. THE HOLY COMMUNION.

This is the highest and most solemn means of grace that a Christian can partake of. This is no common food: it is "the children's bread" —the great spiritual meal, for which God's family from time to time meet around His table. The receiving of the Holy Communion is commonly, especially among the humbler classes, the first *open* act of profession, by which a Christian declares himself to be an earnest follower of his Saviour. It is often the first decided step in the heavenward walk of an awakened person—the first public avowal of his determination to be the Lord's. Now, I must not forget that there are various hindrances, which may often keep back timid Christians.

For instance, you may be afraid of *the strict life*, which an earnest communicant ought to lead; in other words, you may shrink from a close walk with Christ. But is not this what is required of every Christian? To live a holy, and devoted, and self-denying life—this is expected of all Christ's followers; and without it we can be none of His. Oh, fear it not. Shrink not from entering upon it. Doubt not about giving your whole heart to Him. It is your duty, to which you pledged yourself at your baptism. It is your happiness too. You will find it the only way of obtaining real and solid peace.

Or, do those words of the Apostle alarm you, which speak of "*eating and drinking unworthily?*" A humble and earnest Christian, weak though he be, and encompassed with infirmities, is welcome to his Saviour's table. If he comes renouncing all goodness of his own, throwing himself on Christ for acceptance, and earnestly desiring to live unto Him, the Saviour's arms will be thrown open to receive him. Come then, my fellow-Christian, in all your weakness and misery, and you will find that "He giveth power to the faint; and to them that have no might he increaseth strength." Isa. xl. 29.

Or perhaps you may hear it said, that "many go, and are *none the better.*" This is true. But because some abuse so high a privilege, that is no reason why *you* should neglect it. And why is it that the ordinance is unprofitable to them, but because they go in a wrong spirit? If you are really anxious about your soul, and honestly wish to serve Christ, and to grow in meetness for heaven, then I feel sure that it will be your desire to approach in a right frame, and you will not come away unblest.

Some, again, tremble to approach the Table of the Lord, *lest Satan should afterwards enter into them,* as he did into Judas, and then that their latter end should be worse than the first. But this is not the trusting spirit of a Christian who has heartily committed his soul into God's hands: it is doubting His power to keep them. Jesus bids us come; and thus offers to supply us with strength for our onward journey. Oh then, think not that He would ever have made this ordinance to be a trap and a snare to tender consciences, and weak believers. Is it your heart's desire to serve Him? Then do not think so hardly of Him, as to suppose that He could allow that, which He intended for your welfare, to be unto you " an occasion of falling."

Believe me, it is not a matter of small importance, whether you come to this sacrament or stay away. Christ has given it as *a plain command* to His followers to " do this in remembrance" of Him. If then you are one of His servants, or if you have an earnest longing to be one, you will not think lightly of so great an ordinance. You are on your journey to heaven. The way is steep, and the path rugged, and you yourself full of weakness. You need nourishment by the way; and here is the richest food—you are invited to feed spiritually on the body and blood of your Lord.

If you have never approached this heavenly feast, I would counsel you not to be content for one moment longer to turn away from it. You cannot be a true Christian, and yet disobey so plain a command of your Lord. You cannot expect to grow in grace, if you neglect so important a means of grace. Go to your minister, or to some pious friend, and consult him about it. Lay open your difficulties to him, and ask him to guide you in this matter.

But if you are already a Communicant, look upon it as your highest privilege. Try to realize constantly your union with Christ, and "feed upon Him in your heart by faith." His "flesh is meat indeed, and his blood is drink indeed." John vi. 55.

And need I exhort you to be a *regular* communicant? Surely if you have indeed tasted that the Lord is gracious, your very soul will long for this precious feast. You cannot too often wait upon Christ. You cannot be filled too full with His blessings. Your soul needs much; and your Lord has much to give you. Welcome then your Communion Sundays as your best Sundays. Look forward to them with joy and delight. Expect a large blessing from them. And count your admission to the Lord's table as a great honour, of which you are but little deserving.

And that you may get a rich blessing to your soul, let me recommend to you *special preparation* before receiving the holy Communion. Spend a little time, during the few previous days, in solemnizing your heart for this holy ordinance. Make it a time for inward heart-searching, for lifting up the soul to God, and holding closer communion with Him. Why are our sacramental seasons not more profitable? Why have we so often to complain that the ordinance is not more blest to us? It is, I think, because we take so little pains to trim our lamps, and put our hearts in order, for the reception of our Lord and Master. Doubtless He is ready to meet us in His own feast. There He is waiting to cheer us, and feed us, and bless us. But we feel cold and strange in His presence. A musical instrument, even the best, needs careful tuning before it is fit for use. Without this, would it not be folly to attempt to play correctly upon it? And how much more do our hearts require to be tuned before coming to so sacred a feast, and warmed by a nearer intercourse with our heavenly Friend!

The Communicants in a parish are the only persons who in fact claim *full membership* with the Church. Others may *belong* to the Church of England, but these are *in full communion* with her. Others may be in the outer fold; but only these are in the way of feeding upon the full richness of the pasturage.

Count it then your privilege and blessedness

to be numbered among your Saviour's guests. Look upon this feast as the highest means of obtaining His blessing. And although there may be here and there a faithless one among those who approach His table—even as there was a Judas among the twelve—still pray that *you* at least may be found faithful and consistent; and thus there will be no lack of blessing for *you*.

I have now called your attention to the principal *Public* means of grace, which God has ordained for the support and nourishment of the Christian's life. Do not undervalue any one of them. It has been said, that "every ordinance of God is what we make it to ourselves;" that is, its amount of blessing to us depends on our hearts being in a right state to receive it. For instance, one man approaches the Lord's Table carnally and blindly. He eats the bread, and drinks the wine; but there is no Christ there for *him*. By his side, perhaps, there kneels one in penitence and faith. He finds Christ in the ordinance, and feels the truth of that word, "My flesh is meat indeed, and my blood is drink indeed." Again, one man may hear a sermon with his ears, and carry nothing away; he may even attend to it, and understand it, and yet it may never reach his heart; whilst another may hear the self-same sermon, and be aroused by it, or taught by it, or comforted by it.

Oh then, ask God to make you a fit receiver of these means of grace. Ask Him to make His ordinances channels of blessing to you—golden pipes, through which the streams of His grace shall flow into your soul.

CHAPTER IV.

HELPS BY THE WAY

PRIVATE PRAYER AND PRAISE.

BESIDES those *Public* Helps which our heavenly Father has provided for His children, He has also furnished other methods of a more *Private* kind, which they must diligently use, if they would grow in grace. One of these, and perhaps the most important, is PRIVATE PRAYER.

We are again and again charged, in God's word, to engage in this holy exercise. Our Lord himself says, to each one of His followers, "But *thou*, when thou prayest, enter into thy closet; and, when thou hast shut thy door, pray to thy Father which is in secret, and thy Father which seeth in secret shall reward thee openly." (Matt. vi. 6.) When a person is first awakened, there is, as I have said, generally a hungering for public ordinances, especially preaching. But perhaps it is *closet work* that we most need—drawing near to God in secret, and telling out to Him our many wants and deficiencies.

Doubtless, you have often *said* your prayers. You have, perhaps, been accustomed all your life regularly to say prayers morning and evening; but can you not now look back and see that it was but a cold, formal service—the repeating a string of holy words, and but little more? It was *lip*-work, and not *heart*-work. You used words of prayer, but you did not *pray*. You went through the ceremony of certain devotions, as a soldier goes regularly through his exercises, but the *spirit of prayer* was altogether wanting. Alas! you have reason, indeed, to ask God to pardon *this* among your other sins—to forgive the sin you have so often committed *on your knees*.

If, however, you have now a new life within you, *Prayer* will be one sure sign of the change. If the Holy Spirit is at work in your soul, you cannot but pray. When a child is first born, we know that it is a *living* child, because it *breathes*. When a man has been nearly drowned, one of the first symptoms of returning life is that his bosom heaves. And so, if your soul has been quickened by the Spirit of God, and "is passed from death unto life," you will surely breathe the breath of prayer. God has no dumb children: they all cry, "Abba, Father." You may remember that it was said of Saul, when he was converted, "Behold! he prayeth." (Acts ix. 11.) Others might not have seen him pray, but his God did. There he was, concealed from the eyes of men, pouring out his soul before the Lord. Like you, it may be, he had *used prayers* all his life; day after day he had offered up words to God; but never till then did he put up *real prayer*—prayer that came from his heart, prayer that burst forth from a soul deeply conscious of its wants.

Mark this—if you are a true Christian, you will be a *praying* Christian. Many a one has gone to heaven without the advantage of public ordinances; for he may have lain for years on a sick bed, and so have been debarred from them altogether. Some have reached that happy place, without ever being able to read a single page in a book. But never has any Christian struggled through this world, and gained the victory at last, without *prayer;* no, not one. Prayer is absolutely essential to the Christian's life. It is the key, as it were, by which the door of heaven is unlocked. It is the watchword of every Christian soldier.

Christians may differ from one another on many points. Some Christians are rich, and some poor; some are learned, and some have little or no learning; some have many trials, and some have few. But all true Christians are alike in this one thing—they love prayer; they feel the value of it; they pray constantly, and from the heart.

A man need not be a scholar to pray. It is not learning that is needed, but spiritual life and earnestness. It is very possible to have much knowledge of worldly things—yes, and even a head knowledge of religion too—and yet a praying heart may be altogether wanting. It is not so much the words that God regards, as it is the heart that utters them. A cold prayer will be a rejected prayer. There must be fire in the sacrifice, otherwise it will not mount upwards. Earnest cries—heart cries— these take the Lord's ear, and move His compassion; for these are the voice and cries of His own children. A little girl once beautifully described prayer by saying that it was "*the heart talking with God;*" and Luther tells us that it is "*the mind mounting up to Him.*"

Our fluent language, or our well chosen words, will do but little to recommend our devotions to God; it is their being breathed out from the heart. Then every groan speaks, and every word is winged, and reaches the throne on high. "It is not the composition of prayer," says Archbishop Leighton, "or the eloquence of expression, that is the sweetness of it in God's sight, and makes it a sacrifice of a sweet savour to Him, but the breathing forth of the desire of the heart. This it is that makes it a *spiritual* sacrifice; otherwise, it is as carnal, and dead, and worthless, as the carcases of beasts. Therefore David says, 'Let my prayer be set forth as incense; and the lifting up of my hands as the evening sacrifice.'" Psalm cxli. 2.

The man spoken of at page 16, the man who had fallen into a pit, would not require *learning* to enable him to ask for help. The feeling of his danger, and of his wants, would put words into his mouth, and make him earnest in his cries. And so, if you have a pressing sense of your need, you will and must pray.

Depend upon it, dear friend, you cannot love God, and become really acquainted with Him, without often speaking to Him; neither can you overcome the many difficulties of your Christian course, without His help; you cannot win heaven without it.

How is it that we sometimes see so great a difference even among Christians? We see one growing in the knowledge and love of God; making rapid strides towards heaven; meek, and gentle, and Christ-like in his conduct; walking humbly and closely with his God; and recommending religion to others by his holy and happy life. And we see another, perhaps with more talk and profession, but harsh and unloving in his spirit; with a great deal of knowledge, and quick in detecting the wrong in others, but unwatchful and inconsistent in his own walk. He makes no progress in the path of holiness. There is no real growth in grace. But his state to-day is much what it was a year ago.

How is this? What makes the difference between these two? They are both perhaps looking to Christ alone to save them; they both come regularly to God's house, and to God's Table; they both choose God's people as their companions; they both pass for religious persons. What can be the reason then that the one is so true and bright a Christian, and that the other is so deficient? It is that the one is *a praying Christian;* the other too often neglects prayer. The one lives to God, and holds daily and hourly intercourse with Him; the other knows of Him, but lives at a distance from Him.

What unspeakable strength will prayer bring to you! Utterly weak in yourself, you will thus become " strong in the Lord, and in the power of his might." "A man of prayer," says one who is now with God, " is a man of power. A praying soul is a thriving soul. Our great adversary, the devil, is aware of this; he knows full well the secret of our strength. Hence the closet is the Christian's battle-field. There he conquers. Satan aims at this fortress. He triumphs when he has succeeded in baffling prayer: but he 'trembles when he sees the weakest saint upon his knees.' "

Make it your practice *never* to rise in the morning without kneeling down, and engaging, at least for a few minutes, in heartfelt prayer. And *never* think of going to rest at night without doing the same.

I put in the words "kneeling down," because I know that some have the bad habit of saying their prayers in bed. But surely this does not look like drawing near to a great and holy God; this is not the posture in which a sinner should approach Him. I trust that a mere hint on this point will be sufficient.

But prayer twice a-day will not satisfy an earnest soul. The Christian, who is seeking heaven with all his heart, needs to put himself oftener in his Father's presence. He feels that, between morning and evening, the gap is too wide. Hear what David's resolution was—"*Evening*, and *morning*, and at *noon*, will I pray, and cry aloud; and he shall hear my voice." Such, too, was Daniel's habit—"He kneeled upon his knees *three times a day*, and prayed, and gave thanks before God." Possibly you may be so placed, that it may be exceedingly difficult for you to practise such a habit, but make an effort to do so if you can; and you will, indeed, reap a blessing from it. Whether you are in your house, or in the fields, get alone, if possible, for a few minutes, and pour out a word or two of secret prayer to Him, who is watching over you with a Father's love, and is ever ready to meet you with a Father's blessing.

But the Bible bids us "Pray without ceasing." (1 Thess. v. 17.) This means that we should always be *in a prayerful frame:* not always upon our knees; but always waiting upon God, and constantly looking up to Him for grace, guidance, and protection.

I was once asked by a sick person if it was necessary to pray with *a loud voice,* to shew our earnestness. Surely not. A child of God may offer up an acceptable prayer, though he may not be able to speak a word. As in Hannah's case, there may be no utterance, and yet we may pray inwardly. (1 Sam. i. 13.) It is the heart that prays—not the knees, nor the hands, nor even the lips. Have you not seen a dumb man, who stood with his back to the wall, beg as well with his imploring eye and open hand, as one that had a tongue to speak? Our prayers must be as arrows shot from the heart; for none but these will reach the throne of God. "Prayer (says an old writer) is the soul's desire, which God may hear, though it be not expressed in words, for He knows the heart. 'Lord, thou hast heard *the desire* of the humble,' says David. A Christian's *desire* is a real prayer; and words are but the outward clothing of it."

The habit of lifting up our hearts to God *often* during the day is very beneficial, whether this is done silently with our hearts only, or whether we give actual utterance with our lips. Our prayers on these occasions may be short; but God will hear them. Are we, for instance, plunged into some sudden and unexpected danger? we may pray, like the disciples, "Lord, save me; I perish." (Matt. viii. 25.) Are we in any difficulty? we may act like good Nehemiah, who, when spoken to by his sovereign, lifted up his heart to God for direction as to the answer he should give. (Neh. ii. 4.) Or do we at any moment specially feel our weakness? we may use David's words, " Hold thou me up, and I shall be safe." (Ps. cxix. 117.) Or, are we oppressed with an overpowering feeling of our guilt? the Publican's prayer will suit us, " God be merciful to me a sinner." (Luke xviii. 13.) This kind of prayer is called "*ejaculatory prayer.*" And I am sure you will find that the habit of thus darting up short petitions frequently during the day will bring a great blessing with it. It will relieve the soul of its burden. It will call down help when you most need it. It will bring God to your side. It will keep up a constant intercourse between you and your Lord. It will lighten the toils and trials of this world, and sweeten its joys. It will enable you to pass over its rough waves with calmness and safety. But remember this, that "if the arrow of prayer is to enter heaven, it must be drawn from a heart fully bent."

Again, it is important that you should learn to bring *every want* you have, and *every little difficulty* that perplexes you, before your heavenly Father. Hear the direction which St. Paul gives us on this point, "Be careful for nothing (he says), but in *everything* by prayer and supplication, with thanksgiving, let your requests be made known unto God." (Phil. iv. 6.) No want can be *too great* to bring to Him, and no want *too small* to keep back from Him. A person was once asked by a learned infidel, "How great is your God?" She beautifully replied, "He is so great that the heaven of heavens cannot contain Him, and yet so small that He will condescend to dwell in my heart." Of God it may be said, that there is nothing too great for Him to perform, and nothing too small for Him to notice. We know that, whilst He made the stars, and guides them in their courses, He shapes the little dewdrop, and marks even a sparrow's fall. It has been said, "If our cares are too trifling to be carried to God, they are too trifling *to be cares at all.*" Look upon Him, then, as your loving Father; and be often running to Him to tell Him all that concerns you, and to beg Him to guide, direct, strengthen, and help you. This is living a life of prayer. This is the way to know God, to walk with Him, to live upon Him.

> Hast thou within a care so deep
> It chases from thine eyelids sleep?
> To thy Redeemer take that care,
> And change anxiety to Prayer.
>
> Whate'er the care that breaks thy rest,
> Whate'er the wish that swells thy breast,
> Spread before God that wish, that care,
> And change anxiety to Prayer.

Are there not times when you feel, "Oh, that I had a friend, into whose ear I could pour out all my wants, who would feel for me, and wisely counsel me in my various difficulties!" I have shown you that you have just such an one—a loving, tender, wise, powerful Friend, who is ever near you, and who is always ready to hearken to you.

> No human voice may cheer thee,
> No earthly listener hear thee;
> But, oh, one Friend is near thee,
>   The kindest and the best;
> Whose smile can banish sadness,
> Whose presence fills with gladness
>   The solitary breast.

And does it not often happen, that you are in great difficulty how to act in some particular case? Your course is not plain. Your way is not open. Each side seems equally balanced, and you cannot tell which to choose. Your wishes, perhaps, point one way, and your fears another. You are afraid lest you should decide wrongly; lest you should take what may in the end prove hurtful to you, and turn out to be poison; lest the blossoming rod should change into a serpent. It is very trying to be brought into this painful conflict. And it adds to our distress if we are forced to go forward at once, and take one course or the other.

Shall I tell you what to do in such a case? Shall I tell you how you may be sure to find unspeakable relief? Go and lay the matter before the Lord, as Hezekiah did with the King of Assyria's letter. (Is. xxxvii. 14.) Do not, however, deceive yourself, as many do, and seek counsel of God, having already determined to act according to *your own* will, and not according to *His*. But simply and honestly ask that He would guide you. Commit the case to your Father in heaven; and surrender yourself, as a little child, to be led as He pleases. This is the way to be guided aright, and to realize the blessing of having a heavenly Counsellor.

In connexion with prayer, it is no small encouragement to know and feel, that we have an Almighty Pleader, an Advocate, an Intercessor, speaking for us to our heavenly Father. When you pray, Jesus prays for you. When your poor lisping words go up to heaven, your petitions pass, as it were, through His hands, and are accepted for His sake. "He ever liveth to make intercession for you;" and "Whatsoever ye shall ask of the Father, *in His name*, He will give it you." Heb. vii. 25; John xv. 16.

But are we not told that the Holy Spirit intercedes for us also? What then is the difference between His intercession and Christ's? There is this difference—Jesus intercedes for us *in heaven:* the Holy Spirit intercedes for us *within our own hearts.* Jesus pleads our cause in the courts above: the Spirit makes us feel our wants, and fills us with right desires, and thus puts forth His earnest pleadings within our souls.

Perhaps you have found that it is a hard thing to pray aright. It is easy to talk about prayer—easy to urge it upon others—but most difficult to engage in it as I have recommended. I know of nothing which more painfully shows us our infirmity than this, or makes us feel more keenly that we want a helper. We need to be daily taught how to pray. And this is what the Holy Spirit does, by His heavenly influence in our souls. Hear what the apostle says, "Likewise the Spirit also helpeth our infirmities; for we know not what we should pray for as we ought; but the Spirit itself maketh intercession for us with groanings which cannot be uttered." (Rom. viii. 26.) Entreat the Holy Spirit to do this for you. Beg of Him, again and again, to shew you your wants, to give you grace to draw near to God in a right frame, and to enable you to seek only for right things.

And here the question may be asked, "Is it right for a Christian to pray for *temporal* blessings?" Surely it is. Our Lord, in the prayer which He has taught us, has shewn us that this is lawful: for He would have us ask for "our daily bread." But when we ask for any temporal blessing, we should ask for it *in submission to God's will.* Do we, for instance, pray for health? we should at the same time express our willingness to receive sickness, if God should see fit to send it. Or, if we ask that our worldly undertakings may prosper, we should put it in some such way as this—"Give me, O Lord, success, *if* it be for my good, and for Thy glory." Ask almost what you will, *with this proviso,* and you will not be likely to ask amiss.

Another question too may possibly have perplexed you a little—"Is it best to use extempore prayer, or a form?" I have shown that for *public* prayer there is a great advantage in a form; for thus all are aware beforehand what petitions they are about to offer. But in *private* devotion it may well be left to the feeling and judgment of individual Christians. We should approach our heavenly Father in the simplest way, and in a childlike spirit. We should tell out all our wants to Him, and divulge the hidden secrets of our hearts. Now, many feel that this can best be done in their own words. For since no one can repent for another, or believe for another, or know his exact feelings, so no one can supply him with just the words that are suitable to his particular case. Each one has his own special business to transact with God, and no one else can do it for him. But others again have experienced so much difficulty in utterance, that they have found it more profitable to use the words of other men, which, in a general way at least, express their own wants and desires. In either case, we must try and specify every sin for which we need pardon—such as our unbelief and hardness of heart; our want of love to Christ and His people; our uncurbed passions; our unsubdued will; the lustfulness of our thoughts; our hastiness of spirit; the many sins of our tongue; the greediness of our appetite; the peevishness of our temper; our dulness and weariness in the things of God; our want of charity, our evil surmisings, and our evil reportings; and a hundred other sins which, alas, beset us day by day. We should mention also each particular want that we desire to have relieved. And let me again remind you that that prayer only is acceptable to God, which comes direct from the heart, and is offered up in the name of Jesus Christ, the great Intercessor.

Upon the whole, I feel disposed to recommend the following plan—Get a few Headings for Prayer, either written or printed, suitable for each day. And then clothe them in your own words, and enlarge upon them as you may require.

I ought perhaps to say a word or two here about *answers to our prayers.* God's people sometimes pray for spiritual blessings, and then they are disappointed if they are not bestowed. They are almost tempted to think that God has not heard them. But we should never forget, that prayer from the heart is *always* heard; and if the answer is delayed, there is some good reason for it. It is either to humble us more, or to make us value what we ask for, or to try our faith.

Then too we should bear in mind that our prayers *are* often answered, but the answer is overlooked, because it does not come just as, we would have it come. "An answer to prayer" (says a quaint old writer) " does not always come in the way we expect it. We look for it at the fore door, and it comes in at the back door; and while we are still expecting the friend we look for, he is in the house." The mercy we desired is received; only it comes in a way we thought not of, and consequently we are apt to overlook it. Therefore, take heed of confining God to *your* way, or limiting Him to *your* time. His ways are not our ways. You ask, perhaps, for grace to become more holy; and God sends you affliction. Here your petition is granted, but not in the way that you looked for. You ask, again, for the removal of some trial; but, instead of taking it away, God deals with you as He did with St. Paul; He gives you—what is equally good for you—grace to bear the trial. But I must not enlarge upon this.

There is one delightful exercise connected with prayer, which I cannot omit to notice; namely, THANKSGIVING. It may almost be called a part of prayer. This is the apostle's direction, "In everything by prayer and supplication, *with thanksgiving,* let your requests be made known unto God." (Phil. iv. 6.) Praise is far the happiest and pleasantest part of our devotions. No one knew its sweetness better than David. It is remarkable that, out of the one hundred and fifty Psalms, no less than sixty-six are Psalms of *praise*. The five last begin and end with the words, " Praise ye the Lord."

It is sad to think how much more ready we are to sue for blessings, than to express our thankfulness when the boon is granted. We receive the gift, but forget to thank the great and gracious Giver. In the time of trouble, for instance, we go and seek God with some degree of earnestness; but when His heavy hand is taken off us, and the light of His countenance shines once more upon us, then we forget to praise Him. Alas, may it not be said of us, as it was of Israel, " In their *affliction* they will seek me early"? (Hos. v. 15.) And yet how much it becomes the children of God to be thankful. What! shall He show us daily tokens of His love? shall He strew our path with blessings? shall He withhold no good thing from us, not even the gift of His Son? and have we no words of thankfulness to utter His praise? Like the nine Lepers, shall we receive benefits at the hands of Christ, and then return not to give glory to God?

If your conscience tells you that you have been wanting in the work of *praise,* tune up your heart anew for this most sweet and pleasant duty. Try and thank God daily for some one thing at least. Get into the way of daily "counting up your mercies." The very habit will conduce not a little to your happiness. You will be honouring God. And you will be already entering upon that which will be your blessed occupation in heaven.

Dear reader, I would earnestly counsel you to make a firm stand in the duty of secret prayer. Let nothing tempt you ever to neglect it. Never put it by for something else. Never hurry it over, and shorten it, as though you felt that any one thing could be more important than the season of communion with God. It is of all seasons the most precious. "From the few hours we spend in prayer" (says Bishop Taylor), "the return is great and profitable; and what we sow in the minutes and spare portions of a few years, grows up to crowns and sceptres in a happy and glorious eternity."

May you "pray in the Spirit!" May you feel prayer to be more and more delightful to you! May He, who has an ear to hear, ever give you a heart to pray! And may yours indeed be *accepted* prayer!

CHAPTER V.

HELPS BY THE WAY.

THE BIBLE.

THE Word of God is the Christian's daily nourishment. And if he has, indeed, been "born again of the Spirit," he will "desire the sincere milk of the word, that he may grow thereby." (1 Pet. ii. 2.) The "natural man" has no appetite for this heavenly food; but it is sure to spring up in that heart which is renewed by the grace of God.

The Bible is God's book, written by men who "spake as they were moved by the Holy Ghost." Receive that book, then, "not as the word of *men*, but as it is, in truth, the word of *God*." (1 Thess. ii. 13.) Yes, that book which, perhaps, you have so often carelessly read—that book which you have often looked upon as little more than a task-book—that book is *the Word of God.* It contains all that an inquirer after religious truth need know. Here are " the words of eternal life." Here is spiritual food, that can feed, bless, and save you. The Bible is the Guide-post, as it were, to lead poor wanderers to heaven, to point out the way to that " better country " before them. It is the Compass, which shows us, as we pass over the troubled waves of life, how we may reach the wished-for haven. It is the Medicine chest, which contains the only remedy that can cure a diseased soul. It makes known God's will to man. In prayer *we speak to Him ;* but here, in the Bible, *He speaks to us.*

What a blessing it is, that God has given us a book, which lays open to us His will concerning us. Here is something genuine and substantial to depend upon. We can go to our Bibles, and read, " Thus saith the Lord." There are no *perhapses* in this holy volume: it speaks to us with authority. Oh, it is when we read God's Word with the felt impression that it is His message to our souls, that it is sweet indeed to our taste.

No doubt, you have often heard that, in damp and marshy places, it is not uncommon in the night to observe a certain bright appearance in the air, which has sometimes been mistaken for a lantern, or the light from a house. Many a lonely traveller, who has lost his way, has seen this light in the distance. A momentary feeling of joy has come across him; for he has thought within himself, " Surely there is some welcome habitation there, in which I may find a shelter." He has followed the light, but only to get farther from the right road. It has led him into fresh danger, till at last he discovers that he has been following a mere vapour which deceived him.

And is it not thus that Satan sometimes endeavours to mislead us? He tempts us to follow other lights than the true one. He is ever trying to draw us into the wrong road, and then he leaves us in our misery. But, happily, God has given us a sure guide, if we will only follow it. " Thy word " (says David) " is a lamp unto my feet, and a light unto my path." Ps. cxix. 105.

Before we go any farther, I would advise you to ask God's pardon for all your heedless, profitless reading of his Word. Ask Him to forgive you the great sin of an unheeded Bible. And, now make up your mind to take this Word as your companion, and the guide of all your steps, as you journey on to heaven. I have spoken, in the Third Chapter, about *hearing* the Gospel; but I now want to urge you to the careful and devout *reading* of holy Scripture.

1. Read your Bible *daily*—yes, *daily*. I have sometimes found persons, who have been awakened, somewhat backward in this work. They will walk miles to hear a sermon, perhaps. Anything that is a little exciting seems to fall in with their taste. And, meanwhile, they neglect the calm, quiet, and most blessed occupation of searching into the Word of Life, as those who are looking for a hid treasure.

Oh! beware of this evil which so many fall into—even religious persons. Take your empty pitcher, day by day, to this wellspring of life; and, though you may only seem to get a drop now and then, God will be daily filling you out of His fulness. Never let *a single day* pass without reading some portion of Scripture. Your body needs daily food, and so does your soul. Both will suffer without it. You may be pressed for time; you may have scarcely a spare moment that you can call your own. I am aware how busily occupied you sometimes are. Still, I would urge upon you the importance of having, if possible, *a fixed time in every day* for feeding upon this heavenly manna. Read a verse or two only, if you have not time for more. I have known poor men and women, who never miss this their daily meal. I have known men of business in London, who, though pressed with work, set apart a fixed time in every day, for this sacred purpose. And we have all read of a certain King, who had all the affairs of a great nation upon his hands, but who could still say, " Oh, how I love thy law : it is my meditation all the day ;" " Thy testimonies are my delight and my counsellors." (Ps. cxix. 24, 97.) Go, and do thou likewise.

2. Let your Scripture reading be *a solemn work*. Some read the Bible with a lightness, which shows that they can hardly feel its immense value. Now, I would particularly advise you never to take it up carelessly ; and not to be content with reading it just at odd times, when you have nothing else to do, and when you happen to have a few spare moments. This sort of reading is not only unprofitable,

but sometimes actually hurtful. Learn to approach the holy volume with a feeling of reverence and godly fear; and treat it as something too precious to be trifled with.

3. Study the Bible *with prayer*. You may read page after page, but it will be to little profit, unless you get a blessing from above. How would it be with a blind man? Let a book of any kind be placed before him. He might open it, and turn over its pages; but all would be in vain; he would get nothing from it. And *you* are blind—not so blind as you once were—but still you only see dimly. And, unless God says, "Let there be light," there will be none. He must shine upon the Word, and open your heart to receive it.

Whenever you read your Bible, then, pray earnestly for God's teaching. Pray that the Holy Spirit may be given to you, to "guide you into all truth." (John xvi. 13.) Ask God to prepare you to give a cordial welcome to His truth, and so to break up the soil that when you read the word your heart may be like an open furrow, ready to receive into it the precious seed. And then, I am sure, you will find your soul warmed and blest; and the light will grow stronger and stronger within you.

4. Read the Bible in a *teachable and obedient* spirit, as a little child, feeling your ignorance. Say to yourself, when you open the book, " Now I am going to *learn something;* now I am going to draw water from the wells of salvation." Whatever God's Word teaches, *receive it as from Him.*

Our reading and our hearing should produce *some fruit* in us: it should lead to some good result. What is the use of our knowing more about holiness, for instance, unless we become holier persons—of learning that this is right, and that is wrong, unless we set ourselves earnestly to follow the one, and avoid the other—of becoming better acquainted with the history of our Lord, and of His servants; unless we forthwith endeavour to be like them, and to walk as they walked? He who reads only for reading's sake, and without practising what he learns to be God's will, is a mere speculator in religion. But, on the other hand, if, the moment you discover a truth, you immediately set yourself *to act upon it,* then you will have more grace given you to make further advances in the knowledge of God "If any man will *do his will,* he shall know of the doctrine." (John vii. 17.) The

Psalmist speaks of this as the great secret of his growing in knowledge,—"I understand more than the ancients, because I keep thy precepts." Ps. cxix. 100.

Whatever, then, you see commanded in God's word, *go and do it*. Say to yourself, I must forthwith carry this out in my daily life. Do not wait till your conscience grows slack again; but act at once, whilst the feeling of what is right is strong within you. Whatever is written in the Bible, whether it be pleasant or not to your taste, look upon it as something that is *to be obeyed*.

5. Read through *one book of the Bible, before you begin another;* not a chapter in one part to-day, and in another part to-morrow. In this way you will be much more likely to get the meaning of God's word, and to profit by it. If you received a letter from a friend, you would gather but little from it by pitching upon a passage here, or a sentence there. Surely you would read the letter through, if you wished to get a clear view of what it contained. Now, each book of the Bible is like a separate letter; and therefore, instead of taking a chapter at random, you will do well to choose

a gospel, or an epistle, or any other part, and go regularly through it, before you begin another. This you will find the best way of reading Scripture, so as to understand it.

I would not advise you, however, to read a great deal at once. A little, well studied and prayed over, may be as good for your soul as a larger quantity. Sometimes, only a very few verses, thoroughly weighed, will afford you the sweetest nourishment, and will teach you more than whole chapters carelessly read.

6. Have some *settled plan* for your Scripture reading. Read it *methodically*. There should be a plan and method in all we do; and in nothing is this more necessary than in our Bible studies. It is quite possible for a person to be a great reader of God's word, and yet to know but little of its contents. He may get nothing more than a smattering of Scripture. He may fill his memory with Bible phrases and expressions. He may lay hold of certain favourite doctrines, and on these he may dwell with delight, and even with profit. But, after all, this fitful, desultory, kind of reading will give him but a very imperfect knowledge of God's truth—of His truth as a whole.

Now, let me try and assist you in forming a plan. I will suppose that you feel your Scripture reading to have been hitherto very unsatisfactory, and that you are now really desirous to make it more profitable. I will take it for granted that you can, by a little effort, find time for *two* readings during each day.

I would recommend you then to take, in the morning, some part of the *Old* Testament. And let your first act be to lift up your heart to God for His teaching. You might use some such short prayer as this:—" Give me, O Lord, thy Holy Spirit to enlighten my blindness. Teach me out of thine own word, and write thy truth in my heart, for Jesus Christ's sake." Then open your Bible with the feeling that there is some holy lesson to be learnt from it, some truth to be found which shall give fresh light to your soul. You are beginning, perhaps, the Book of Genesis, or Proverbs, or Isaiah. It is well first to consider what sort of a book it is you are going to study. Is it the history of the Lord's dealings with His people of old? Then try and cull from it something to warn you, or to encourage you. Does it contain precepts for your guidance? Feel that every word is *for you;* and make a resolution that what you read shall, by God's grace, influence your conduct. Or is it a prophecy ? Then expect to meet with something dark and difficult, and much to call out your faith. Do not read a great deal; but what you do read, read well and thoughtfully.

In the evening, again, you may be able to set apart a little time for this blessed study; and then it may be well to read a portion of the *New* Testament. But let it be a fixed and regular portion. If you are going through one of the Gospels, remember that you are reading what the Son of God himself did and said. Study His spotless and holy character, and make it your pattern. And when you think of all that He endured—the coldness, the ill-treatment, the unbelief, the contempt, the contradiction of sinners, the untold agonies that He met with—bear in mind that all this was *for you*, and in order that He might be the great Sin-bearer, and Sorrow-bearer, of a fallen world. Or, if you read the Acts of the Apostles, you will find it very good for you to trace the course of those early followers of Christ, who counted not their lives dear unto themselves, so that they might bear the Saviour's cross after Him here, and wear His crown hereafter. Or, if you are reading one of the Epistles, consider the circumstances under which the particular Epistle, or Letter, was sent; by whom it was written; and to what body of Christians, or to what person among them, it was addressed; and endeavour to look upon each verse as though it contained a message of God to your own soul.

As to *the quantity* we should read, it must depend much on the time we have, the state of our mind, our wants, &c. Some Christians find it very beneficial, now and then, to take a short passage, and to break it up, as it were, so as to examine every expression and every word separately; and thus endeavour to extract from it all the sweetness that it contains. Some, too, have found a great advantage from the habit of stopping occasionally, and turning Scripture into prayer, thus making it a devotional exercise.

In any case, the fault of most readers of Scripture is that they do not sufficiently meditate upon it, and turn it over in their minds, and digest it as they do the food that nourishes their bodies. When they have read a chapter or two, they are apt to look upon it *as a thing done;* and the subject they have been dwelling upon is allowed altogether to pass away from their minds " as a tale that is told."

Never read for the sake of feeling afterwards that you have *accomplished a task*. For what will it profit you to have run over with your eye a certain number of verses, if, like the Butterfly which flits from flower to flower, you have scarcely gathered any nourishment? Be rather like the Bee, which rests awhile, and draws out the sweetness which lies deep within.

Read Scripture thus thoughtfully, prayerfully, and methodically; and sure I am that God will make it a blessed study to you. It was said of Apollos that he was " mighty in the Scriptures." May the same be said of you! Try to become so. If you do indeed love your Bible, thank God for it. If not, *ask Him to make you love it*. And rest not until you can feel something of David's experience when he said, " How sweet are thy words unto my taste. Yea, sweeter than honey to my mouth! they are the rejoicing of my heart!" Ps. cxix. 103, 111.

CHAPTER VI.

HELPS BY THE WAY.

RELIGIOUS BOOKS.—RELIGIOUS INTERCOURSE.—MEDITATION.—COMMUNION WITH GOD.—SELF-EXAMINATION.

I. RELIGIOUS BOOKS.

THE Bible is not the only book the Christian has to help him on his way. It is the Great Book—the Book of books—the only book that can be called *The Book of God*—the only book which speaks with full authority, and against which there is no appeal. Still, there are other books, which may help you on your way heavenward. And never was there a time, when so many of these helps were placed within our reach. There are books suited to every stage of the believer's experience. This very book which you are now reading is, I hope, one of them. I have tried to suit it to *your* case, my dear reader. May there be, here and there, a remark in it likely to assist you in your great spiritual enterprise.

As the Bible is like *God's own voice* speaking to us, so good books are like *pious friends* conversing with us. They contain many hints, and point out to us many dangers, and give us many encouragements. Be thankful then, when any really good book comes into your possession, or is lent to you for a time. Read it carefully and thoughtfully, and perhaps you may gain from it some profitable knowledge.

If you have leisure, allot some portion of time in each day to this kind of reading. Do not allow yourself to get into the habit of taking up any book which may chance to fall in your way. Such study will do you no good; it will only waste your time. But read something that is really likely to strengthen your mind, warm your heart, and give you clearer and sounder views of God's truth. It will be well to ask your minister, or some wise and godly friend, to counsel you as to what books you should read.

But in taking up any religious book, remember it is only *man's* work. There may be a great deal of good in it, and yet some wrong things in it. The writer may earnestly desire to lead you right, and yet he may possibly be mistaken on some points himself. Try then and cull out what is good from the book you are reading. In the Bible *all* is pure gold; but in other books, even the best of them, there is a mixture of dross with the precious metal.

For instance, a book is lent to you, which contains some very useful advice, and you read it with much benefit to your soul. But perhaps you come to a passage which contains a different view of some particular doctrine from that which you have learnt from the word of God, or from your minister. Now, are you to embrace at once this new view, merely because you find it in a printed book? Certainly not. You would be wrong in allowing your mind to be so easily warped.

Or, again, perhaps a book may fall into your hands, written by some one who is not a member of the Church of England. There may be much true piety in it, and much that is likely to raise your heart upwards. But as you read on, you are suddenly startled by some strong expressions against your Church. The rest of the book may have seemed so true and so sound that you may be half disposed to be led away by the arguments that are used. But bear this in mind—they are merely the words of a man, and there you will find dross mixed with the gold. The writer may be a good man, and yet liable to be mistaken on some points; for even those among us, who have the clearest sight, "only see through a glass darkly"—they only "know in part." (1 Cor. xiii. 12.) Weigh well, then, what you read. And take care, lest a few well-written sentences throw you off your balance, and move you away from the safe ground on which you are standing.

Above all, let no book, however excellent, take the place of *the Book of books.* Man's words must not be valued like God's word. What are common stones in comparison to rubies? "What is the chaff to the wheat?" A religious book, or tract, may very likely put many things before us in a plainer way than the Bible does. But it is a dangerous sign when a person allows these to become his chief study, whilst God's word is laid aside. It was said of Henry Martyn—"So deep was his veneration for the word of God, that when a suspicion arose in his mind, that any other book he might be studying was about to gain an undue influence over his affections, he instantly laid it aside; nor would he resume it, till he had felt and realized the paramount excellence of God's Word. He could not rest satisfied till all those lesser lights, that were beginning to dazzle him, had disappeared before the brightness and glory of the Scriptures."

And now, I am going to mention another staff of a similar kind, from which you may derive some help; but you must not lean upon it too constantly. I mean

II. INTERCOURSE WITH RELIGIOUS FRIENDS.

A person, when first led to think seriously, feels himself to be in a new world; and often times he seems to stand alone, and longs for some Christian friend to help him. I have already shown you to whom you should flee for advice. It is to your clergyman especially you should ever turn for spiritual counsel and comfort. But besides your minister, a friend or two in your own rank of life will be of great use to you. If then you are acquainted with any earnest persons in your parish—among the communicants, for instance —try and get a word with them, and choose such for your closest companions. You may find them of the greatest assistance to you, just as Aquila and Priscilla were to Apollos. (Acts xviii. 26.) Their Christian counsel, their example, their faith, will cheer and encourage you; for as " iron sharpeneth iron, so sharpeneth a man the countenance of his friend." Prov. xxvii. 17.

In speaking to others of God's dealings with us, there is something that warms the heart. And such Christian converse is pleasing to God. "They that feared the Lord" (says Malachi) "spake often one to another: and the Lord hearkened and heard it, and a book of remembrance was written before him for them that feared the Lord, and that thought upon his name. And they shall be mine, saith the Lord of hosts, in that day when I make up my jewels." Mal. iii. 16, 17.

It is a great happiness to enjoy the friendship of one or two really religious persons. As you tell them of the various wants, and difficulties, and doubts, and trials, which have at times almost weighed you down, perhaps you will be consoled and encouraged, by finding that they too have passed through the very same rugged ways in their Christian journey. Many a newly-awakened Christian feels as though no one could have experienced the same religious difficulties and temptations as himself, until he unbosoms his heart to his spiritual teacher, or to some Christian brother; and then he learns to his comfort that his own case is far from being a solitary one.

There is another way in which a really faithful and religious friend may be of much use to you—he may point out to you your faults, faults perhaps which you would not of yourself discover. "Two are better than one," says Solomon; and if you are both travelling on the same blessed road, you may thus give one another much seasonable help by the way. He may assist you, too, in the understanding of many things, which you could not see clearly when alone. He may not be a learned person, and may need to be taught himself; but still he may know much which you have no knowledge of. Or you may be able in your turn to impart to him something, which you have had an opportunity of learning. And so you may give each other a helping hand.

But if you are young in years, or young in

grace, do not forget that your most proper place is that of *a learner*, and not an instructor. It is true, you know more than you once knew; for light has shone in upon your soul. But Satan will perhaps now endeavour to make you think that you know all, and that you must forthwith begin to instruct others. Beware of falling into this snare. Many have done so to their cost. They become proud and forward, when they ought to be modest and retiring. They want to lead others, even before they have learnt to walk themselves. They desire to be spiritual nurses, whilst they themselves are but babes in Christ. Be content to *receive* instruction for a while. You need it; for you have much, very much, to learn. Think more just now of carrying your empty pitcher to the well, than of pouring it out to refresh others. You have yet, I say, much to learn. You are at present like the man mentioned by St. Mark (chap. viii.), who, though cured of his blindness by the Saviour's touch, at first "looked up and said, I see men, as trees, walking." And if you as yet see only a little, do not fall into the error of thinking that you see all. Be backward and diffident in giving advice to others; but be always anxious to receive it yourself—according to the apostle's counsel, "Be swift to *hear,* slow to *speak.*" James i. 19.

I would also caution you against being too free in speaking to every one about the working of your own heart. A little reserve is necessary on this point. Well is it to unbosom our feelings to *a Christian Friend;* but they are too sacred to be laid open to the gaze of *all.* If God's grace is really at work in our souls, there will most likely be a shrinking at first from a public announcement of it: it will declare itself by our altered conduct, rather than by our words.

But there is another "help" that I would strongly advise you not to neglect, and that is—

III. MEDITATION.

Good and helpful as Christian converse is, we *may* become too fond of it, and rely upon it too much. Persons when they first become religious are apt to crave after *intercourse with others.* I have observed this to be an error, into which many of God's people fall. But surely it is very important for us frequently to get by ourselves, and *think.* A person who is always hearing and conversing, is like one who is for ever eating, but never digests his food. And what is the consequence? His health suffers, and what he takes in does him little or no good. And so it is with our spiritual state.

Get into the way then of *meditating* on heavenly things. *Think over* the last sermon that you heard, and let your thoughts dwell upon it; or the last chapter you read in the Bible. Or take some one particular subject, and ponder it well in your mind— such as the goodness of God, or the joys of heaven, or the love of Christ, or the perfectness of His character. You can do this when you are at work, or walking along the road, or sitting in your house. You will find it a little difficult at first, for it is no easy matter to keep your thoughts within bounds; but you will soon acquire the habit, if you persevere.

There is another kind of meditation, too, which is very profitable—holding converse with our own hearts. David spoke of this, when he said, " Commune with your own heart, and be still; " and again, " I commune with mine own heart; and my spirit made diligent search." (Ps. iv. 4; lxxvii. 6.) And whilst we are "thus musing," the fire will oftentimes burn; our hearts will glow; and our love, and faith, and thankfulness, will be increased.

Holy men have always made meditation a

part of their religious exercises; and they embraced the most favourable opportunities for this devout practice. Isaac went out into the field to meditate in the stillness of the evening. David sometimes selected the morning; and at other times, he chose the night, when all was still around him; "I remember thee *upon my bed*, and meditate on thee in the night watches." Ps. lxiii. 6.

IV. COMMUNION WITH GOD.

When we meditate on holy things, we turn them over in our minds, and dwell on them in our thoughts. But besides this, we should hold actual converse with our heavenly Father. This is what I mean by *Communion with God*. It is a most delightful and profitable exercise for the Christian's soul. It is good for him to hold converse with God, to speak with Him as with a Friend, to walk with Him as Enoch did. It draws down constant blessings from above. A plant in your garden may be refreshed for a while by a sudden shower from the waterpot; but it is the gentle dew from heaven, descending morning after morning upon it, that will make it really thrive and grow. So it is with our souls: we must be daily putting ourselves in the Lord's presence, and receiving fresh supplies of grace out of His fulness, or there will be no real progress.

Observe how constantly David and other holy men were engaged in this holy exercise. They were continually lifting up their souls to God. And if you follow their example, you also will succeed in this heavenly employment.

V. SELF-EXAMINATION.

"Examine yourselves, whether ye be in the faith; prove your own selves," was the advice addressed by St. Paul to the Christians at Corinth. (2 Cor. xiii. 5.) And this is a most important means of spiritual health and growth.

When any one first begins to live a religious life, he may perhaps fancy that he is fully acquainted with his own heart. It seems to lie all open before him. But the more he looks into it, the more astonished he will be to find how little he as yet knows of it. Self-examination is therefore most necessary. For how can we become acquainted with our own state, unless we look closely into it? How can we discover our particular failings, our shortcomings, our secret transgressions, our heart-sins, unless we search after them? Without this, our prayers will be nothing more than *general* acknowledgments of guilt, and *general* petitions for pardon and grace. Nothing will be *specified*, because nothing will be known of our exact condition, or of our particular wants.

It has been observed, that "a person, ignorant of his own heart, is like a merchant who knows not the state of his accounts, while every day likely to become a bankrupt; or like persons in a leaky ship, who are not aware of their danger. The professed follower of Christ, who knows not whether he is a true or false disciple, is in a condition no less dangerous."

But you will find it no easy matter to lay bare your own heart. Far easier is it to detect and fix upon the faults of others, than to discover and bring to light your own. Far easier is it to discern the little mote that is in thy brother's eye, than to pull out the huge beam from thine own, or even to feel that it is there. Some sins there are too in most of us, which lie so deeply embedded that, unless we follow them up, and drag them from their hiding-places, they will still hold their ground, and in the end overpower us.

The heart then must be searched—searched to the very core. The deepest recesses of it must be sounded. Everyone should know how things are going on in his soul; what his dangers are; and what are the temptations to which he is most exposed. When an army of soldiers is encamped, the General places sentinels in all directions, whose duty it is to give notice of any attack threatened by the enemy, and to sound an alarm. *Self-examination* is the Christian's sentinel. It watches to see how things are going on in the heart, and it gives notice of attacks from the great Enemy, who is ever on the alert to assault us.

You will find, as I have said, this exercise a little difficult at first. Your sluggish heart will rebel against it. "It is no easy work (says an American writer) to bring a man and his own heart together." But it will soon become less irksome. Only make trial of it, and I am sure you will find it to be no small help to you. Appoint some fixed time in every day, or in every week, for the catechising of your own heart, for unveiling it, and for bringing its hidden things to light; and also for scrutinizing the daily actions of your outer life.

But you will perhaps say that there is a kind of self-examination *always* going on in the mind of a true Christian. Is he not constantly feeling sin within him, and questioning himself whether a thing be right or wrong? Yes; but he wants something more. He needs regular stated seasons for bringing himself to trial; and without this, I believe, he will make little or no advance in the way of holiness.

My advice to you then is, at once to begin the practice of Self-examination. But, if your mind has been unused to the task, it is well not to overtax it at first. You had better begin by asking yourself only a *few* questions. Do not lay upon yourself too heavy a burden at starting, lest you grow weary, and give up what you have begun. It has been remarked that young believers are very much in the condition of persons recovering from illness, whose strength is little, and resolution weak. We would not, therefore, put too heavy a yoke upon them, in this or any other duty, but would have them get on by degrees, as they are able to bear it. And remember, it is written for our encouragement, that God "despiseth not the day of small things."

Of this I am certain, that self-examination, however toilsome, will amply repay you. It will make you watchful; it will keep your lamp burning brightly; it will make you alive to your weaknesses, and lead you to seek earnestly for grace to overcome them; it will enable you, perhaps, to nip many a dangerous sin in the bud; it will save you many a painful pang of conscience, and promote your peace. Above all, it will prepare you for the great Judgment-day. Is it not far better, think you, to discover your besetting sins, one by one, *now;* to mourn over them; to confess them to God; and to lay them out before the cross; than to go on in a state of blindness as to their very existence, and to have them brought against you at that day? "It is better," says Bishop Taylor, "to examine the conscience *now*, while there is time for repentance and amendment, than to be suddenly awakened on a death-bed to the recollection of our sins, when it is too late to alter." Oh, give yourself heartily to this work. Pray, " Search me, O God, and know my heart, and see if there be any wicked way in me, and lead me in the way everlasting." (Ps. cxxxix. 23, 24.) " Let a man examine himself." 1 Cor. xi. 28.

Does any reader say, " I see plainly that this is my duty. But how am I to set about it? when shall I begin? what course shall I follow?" Let me endeavour to help you.

First, if Self-examination is a plain duty,

there should be *no delay* in setting about it. Begin it now—to-day.

Next, as to *how often* it is to be done. Some Christians think it right to examine themselves *daily*. It was the maxim of a heathen philosopher, " Let not thine eyes decline in pleasant sleep, until thou hast recounted all the acts of the long day." Others prefer doing so *once a week*. If the latter, you might take Saturday or Sunday evening, as a suitable time for this exercise. But it is *very* important to have a *fixed, stated* time, or it will be poorly done.

Then, as to *how* you are to examine yourself. I would say, look deep into your heart, and try to discover its actual state before God. Go carefully into your different actions, and words, and feelings, and motives; and weigh them well, so as to discover what has been right, and what has been wrong in you. Let nothing be hidden from yourself, or kept back from God.

There are many books which would help you greatly in the matter. But, in case you should not be able to obtain one of these, I will give you here some few general hints for your guidance :—

1. Examine yourself by the rule of *God's Word*, and not by *man's opinions*. A thing may not be counted wrong by men, and yet God's Word may condemn it.

2. Look not merely at the actions you are daily doing, but inquire from what *motive* they are done. Is it, for instance, from a desire for man's praise; or for worldly gain; or for God's glory?

3. Enquire closely if you have good grounds for believing that you are accepted in Christ, and therefore safe in His hands.

4. If you are Christ's servant, are you bringing forth much fruit? Are you daily growing and advancing in grace?

5. Find out what is your *besetting sin*, as pride, uncharitableness, lust, worldliness, evil temper, &c. Also, whether you are earnestly resolved to thrust it away at any cost.

6. See if you are using self-denial, and ever keeping " the flesh subdued to the Spirit."

7. Find out, not only the actual wrong that you have done, but also the good that you have left undone.

8. Look carefully into every thought, word, and desire.

9. See whether you are taking Christ for your example in all you do.

10. Inquire into your conduct towards your relations, friends, neighbours, masters, servants, &c.

11. Find out to what peculiar temptations you are most liable; in what places, and in what company, they commonly assault you; and prayerfully guard against them.

12. Examine yourself as to whether your bible-reading and devotions are a delight to you, and whether they are regular and solemn, or hurried and trifling.

13. Ask yourself if you are doing *all you might do* for the glory of God, and for the good of your fellow-men.

Above all, ask God to help you in thus searching into your heart. (Psalm cxix. 59; cxxxix. 23, 24.)

In these three chapters, then, I have mentioned some of the means by which you may attain to that holiness "without which no man shall see the Lord." Use them with diligence and thankfulness; and may they help you much in running the race that is set before you!

CHAPTER VII.

CHURCH MEMBERSHIP.

THINK not, O Christian, that thou art a solitary being, standing alone in the midst of this wide world. No; thou belongest to a great spiritual Body, which is called "the Church of God," or "the Church of Christ."

Strictly speaking, those only belong to this blessed Family who are *really and truly Christ's People;* who are under the influence of His grace, are led by His Spirit, and are faithfully serving Him. And of this Body He himself is the living Head. Eph. i. 22, 23; v. 23; Col. i. 18.

But this expression, "the Church," is often used in a much wider sense, to include *all baptized persons.* It is with us Christians much as it was with the Jews of old. They, as a nation, were God's Church. They were also called "a *holy* people," and yet the *really* holy ones among them were but a little flock; for as the apostle says, "They are not all Israel, which are of Israel." Rom. ix. 6.

"The Church on earth," says Bishop Beveridge, "is like a floor, in which the chaff is mixed with the grain; it is like a field, in which the tares and wheat are found: it is like a net, in which are gathered fishes of every kind, both bad and good."

Now, you and I have by baptism been grafted into this Body. We have been numbered among Christ's flock, and placed under His sheltering care. But are we truly His? Are we His *in heart and life*, as well as *in name?* If so, then indeed are our "names written in heaven;" the Lord's mark is upon us, and He will presently take us into His Church above. And there we shall join our dear brethren, whose warfare is over—such as Moses, and Daniel, and Paul, and Stephen, and all those holy ones, who have "washed their robes, and made them white in the blood of the Lamb."

> "One family we dwell in Him,
> One Church above, beneath;
> Though now divided by the stream,
> The narrow stream of death."

But besides belonging to that vast Body, which is spread all over the world, *you* are probably also a member of that lesser company which is called *the Church of England.*

Now, what is the Church of England? Where did it spring from? Is it a true Church? Are we right in belonging to it? I will answer these questions by a very plain and simple illustration.

We will picture to ourselves some wide and noble River, flowing along for miles and miles, far beyond where our eye can reach. Here and there is a little stream branching out from it—a part of the same mighty river—but running in a different channel, and making glad the land through which it flows. Some of these little streams are clear and pure: others are choked up and muddy. Some have pursued their course for years: others have only lately swelled into their present dimensions.

Now, let this main river serve to represent to you the Church of God—the Church which has existed from the days of Christ, or rather from the time of Adam, and Abel, and Enoch; for God has *always* had a people to himself on the earth—that Church for which the Saviour died, and which is so unspeakably dear to

Him, which has lasted, and will last, for ever.

And these little outlets—these little daughter-streams—what do they represent? Why, they are like the various Churches, which have branched out from the parent Body. Some of these are pure Churches, and the favour of God rests upon them: others are impure, and therefore cannot last.

The Churches of *Corinth*, and of *Galatia*, and of *Ephesus*, &c., were all different branches of the one Universal Church. So it is with our own Church. A Branch from that river soon found its way into England. It met with many impediments and barriers at first. Gradually however it forced a passage for itself, causing idolatry and misery to disappear before it, and refreshing and fertilizing the country, wherever its waters found their way. But Satan, who is ever jealous of what interferes with his own designs, soon dropped his seeds of error into this stream, which he hoped would in due time spring up, and produce a large crop of noxious weeds, and so choke it and stop its course. He was, alas, but too successful; and the waters were, for a while, corrupted and checked. I am speaking of the time when

Popery nearly destroyed our Church. Thank God, however, the Reformation came to purify it. The waters were cleansed; the weeds were uprooted and cast away; and once more did the stream flow clear and free. Now again did those who dwelt on its banks bring their vessels, and drink of the pure waters of salvation.

Since then, indeed, Satan has again and again tried to pollute this stream, and to stay its progress. But it seems now to run more freely than ever. It is not only fertilizing our own country; but this little Branch of the great river has reached many a distant land, where it is carrying the richest and choicest blessings.

And now, to leave our illustration, let us see what great reasons we have to be thankful that we are members of the Church of England. I will just mention three.

First, she is a *pure and sound* Church. She is not resting on the shifting opinions of man, but upon God's eternal truth. Her's are the "old paths, where is the good way." In the main, she is the same to-day as she was seventeen hundred years ago, when England first became a Christian country. She honours the Saviour, and leads her children to Him. Therefore, whatever her foes may say—whatever faults and failings they may find in her—she is a safe home for all who seek shelter in her communion, and faithfully follow her teaching as she follows Christ.

Doubtless the Church of England has failings; for what Church has not? Even those that were planted in the days of the apostles were not altogether free from them. False doctrine worked its way into the Church of Galatia: and objectionable practices, and party feeling, into the Church of Corinth. If we look for perfection in any Church on earth, we shall only be disappointed. We must wait for that in the Church above. Meanwhile, be thankful that your Church's faults are so few, and that her excellencies are so many.

Secondly, our Church is a *scriptural* Church. She specially honours the Bible by the large portions of it which she appoints for her services. Her framework too is after the model of God's word. The doctrines which she sets forth can be proved from the Bible. She plainly declares, that " Holy Scripture containeth all things necessary to salvation; so that whatsoever is not read therein, nor may be proved thereby, is not to be required of any man that it should be believed as an article of the faith, or be thought requisite or necessary to salvation." (Article vi.) Those holy men, who drew up our formularies, took the Bible as their guide. And I know of no prayers so enriched with the language of Scripture, and so truly spiritual, as those which are appointed for our public worship. Many pious Dissenters have acknowledged this. "I believe," says Wesley, "there is no Liturgy in the world which breathes more of a solid, scriptural, rational piety, than the Common Prayer-book of the Church of England."

Thirdly, ours is a Church which *meets the wants of all*. It is one of the glories of this Christian country that, from one end of the land to the other, buildings devoted to God's especial service rear their venerable heads. Here the rich and poor meet together, and God is the Maker of them all. Here the humblest, as well as the greatest, may join with his brethren in prayer—prayer that he can understand—prayer suited to his wants— prayer in which he can follow his minister. And here, too, he can sit and listen to the glad sounds of Gospel grace and mercy.

And to each parish there is an appointed Pastor, as well as a House of prayer—not only a safe Fold into which you may be gathered, but a Shepherd to feed you there—one commissioned by God to instruct you, to warn you, to encourage you on your heavenward road, to visit you in your homes, as your spiritual friend and counsellor, and to stand by you in the hour of sickness, and speak to you in the Saviour's name, and tell you of a Saviour's love.

And if your minister should prove faithless to his flock, what then? To his own Master he must stand or fall. But, even in such a case (and, thank God, it is not a common one in these days), you would be wrong to forsake the sound and scriptural Body, to which you are happily united. And yet how often, and how thoughtlessly, this is done! Learn rather to distrust yourself in these matters; and desire rather to be a Learner than a Judge. Because your minister seems to you to be unworthy of his high office, or because you may have taken offence at something that he has said or done, or because his views are not such as to fall in with your own, are you justified in quitting the Church of which you are a member, and seeking for yourself another communion? As well might a soldier desert his company, because the manner in which his captain commanded it was not according to his taste. Rather is it your duty, in such a case, to pray earnestly to God to send you "faithful and true pastors," and, meanwhile, to wait in hope, till He sees fit, in his love, to bring about a happier state of things.

I have not unfrequently observed this—that where a truly Christian man or woman has been living for a while in a parish which is but little cared for, he has, in spite of his disadvantages, grown in grace and humility, from the fact of being thrown more entirely upon the precious teaching of God himself; just as one has sometimes found the sweetest and loveliest flowers growing in some waste and barren spot, uncared for and uncultivated by the hand of man.

Let your love to your Church, then, be independent of the conduct of any one particular Minister. Let your attachment to her be so deeply seated that nothing of the kind which I have spoken of could cause you to separate from her.

I have dwelt a little on this subject, because I think that we are apt to be blind to our duties, and to undervalue our privileges, as Churchmen; and also because there are many who are ever ready to lead away those who seem to be in earnest about their souls, from the fold in which God has placed them.

Now for a word or two of advice.

1. Try and *realize your Church-membership.* Once you were a Churchman, because perhaps your father and mother were so before you. But I hope you will now feel that you have stronger reasons than this. Once you were content with the mere *name;* but now, I trust, you desire to *act* as a Churchman. For just as each member of a *Family* has certain duties to perform to his parent, or his brother, or his sister, so have we all many sacred duties to discharge to our *Church.* We should look upon our fellow-members as beloved brethren in Christ, banded together in the same holy fellowship. We should feel a hearty love for our Church, stand up for it against all opponents, faithfully obey its rules, do our best to promote its interests, and bring as many as we can into its safe and happy fold.

2. Endeavour to be *an active, earnest, and zealous Churchman.* There are many drones in the hive. What we want is men and women who will work heartily for God. You may be but a very humble member of the Church; but still you *are* a member. There is a work then for you to do; yes, a special work. Has not every limb of the body a fixed employ-

ment? Is it only the hands, and the feet, and the tongue, that need act? Surely every separate member of the body must do its part. And so it is also with the Christian body. 1 Cor. xii.

Now, remember this. And ask God to shew you what He would have you to do. Consult your minister, as to how you may best serve Christ, who is your spiritual Head; and then determine no longer to live unto yourself, as perhaps you have hitherto done, but unto Him who loved you, and gave Himself for you.

3. Make yourself more fully *acquainted with the doctrines of your Church*. Read over, carefully and often, the Thirty-nine Articles, which you will find in your Prayer-book, and compare them with God's Word. Then will you have some good reason to give to those who ask you *why* you are a Churchman.

4. Never allow yourself to *speak harshly of those who differ from you*. We should deal by others as we would be dealt by. Our attachment to our own Church ought to be warm and hearty. We should hold our own firmly. And, if so, our hearts will naturally be drawn more closely towards those of our own communion than towards any others. We may feel that those who are not Churchmen are great losers, and that

ours is "the more excellent way." We may be persuaded that *we* are right, and that *they* are wrong. We may feel that schism is a sin; that our Lord would have us all to be one; and that those who "cause divisions" in His Church are weakening it, and thereby grieving Him. But still, however decided we may be in maintaining what we believe to be right, let us never speak one harsh or unchristian word against those who see not as we see. If they love the Saviour, let us love them for His sake; and let us earnestly pray that the time may speedily come, when Christ's people shall be all one; when "Ephraim shall not envy Judah, and Judah shall not vex Ephraim:" but there shall be "one fold and one Shepherd."

There may be some persons who will endeavour to shake your attachment to the Church to which you belong. The moment they see you religiously disposed, they will try to win you over to their own particular party. A really religious Dissenter would scorn to do this. But there are some who, instead of rejoicing to see you on *the Lord's* side, are only anxious to get you on *their* side. They will tell you that you will get more spiritual help with them; that you will meet with a warmer and more brotherly welcome; that you will find, in this or that sect, more pasturage for your soul than you can get in the Church.

Believe it not. God can, and will, bless you in your present communion, if you are faithful to Him. If any would draw you from it, tell them that you dare not leave it : you feel it to be your shelter and your home—a *Pathway of Safety*, which has already led thousands to heaven, and which is able to lead you.

I will now close this chapter in the words of a Christian writer :—" For my own part (he says) I have looked anxiously into the character and working of many systems of religion; and I trust that I know how to respect those who cannot see with my eyes. But, after all my searchings, I find no Church like the old one. I love the shade of the old vine, and the shelter of the old wall, within which my fathers lived well, and died happily. It is delightful to me, in a shifting, fleeting, dying world, to find something which lasts. And I trust, through God's infinite grace, to be a humble, watchful, loving worshipper in this happy company of the Lord's people, till I change the Church on earth for the Church in heaven."

CHAPTER VIII.

DANGERS FROM WITHOUT.

THE WORLD. — LOOSE AND UNGODLY FRIENDSHIPS. — PERSECUTION.

If you have ever read Bunyan's "Pilgrim's Progress," you will remember that "Christian" had not a very easy path on his way to the "celestial city." He had to toil up many a hill, and to encounter many a danger, as he journeyed onward. And so, dear reader, must it be with you and me. If we would "enter the kingdom," it must be "through much tribulation." The way is "narrow" along which we must travel, and the gate "strait" through which we must pass.

Some of these dangers I am going to set before you in this and the next chapter. Not that I would wish to alarm or discourage you. God forbid! But I should be but a poor guide, if, whilst I pointed out to you *the pathway of safety*, I did not tell you of the dangers on every side, and shew you how to meet them. It has been truly said, that " to be *fore*warned is to be *fore*armed."

1. One of your chief dangers will be from THE WORLD. How should you feel and act towards it? You have perhaps hitherto loved the world. Its ways, its pleasures, and its followers, have been all to your taste. The word of God cautioned you, " Love not the world;" but you *did* love it; for you had nothing better on which to set your affections. But now a purer love fills your heart —the love of God—the love of that dear Saviour, of whom you can say, " He is all my salvation and all my desire." If He has indeed taken up his abode within you, then sure I am that there is no longer any room for the world; and much, that once was so sweet to you, you have now no relish for.

" How then am I to act?" you will ask. " Am I to flee from my fellow-men? Am I to give up the occupations of life? Must I run out of the world, as I would escape from some plague-house? Must I wander afar off, and remain in the wilderness? Must I lead a hermit-life? Is this the only way to escape 'the pollutions that are in the world?'" Many have done so, and yet the world has followed them to their lonely cells. In our Lord's last prayer for his people, we see that He would have them *kept in the world*, and yet *preserved from the evil* of it. "I pray not (He says) that thou shouldest take them out of the world, but that thou shouldest keep them from the evil." (John xvii. 15.) He would not have them run away from the world, as from an enemy which they could not master; but He asks for them that God would keep them safely whilst they are in it, and that He would deliver them from its many entanglements.

Whilst, then, you are *in* the world, take care that you are not *of* the world. Try and live above it. If you were dressed in a garment of pure white, and you had to travel along some miry road, would you not walk carefully, picking your way at every step, lest you should soil your snow-white robes? Or if you were passing through a city, where some dreadful and infectious disease existed, would you not be careful to avoid those streets where the disease was raging? Act so with the world. While you mix in its needful employments, endeavour to avoid its snares, and "keep yourself unspotted from the world."

If, for example, you are *a Poor man or woman,* you must needs follow the worldly occupation allotted to you. This is your duty, and you should try and discharge it with honest industry. Endeavour to avoid a worldly spirit. And let your one great aim be to glorify God in your humble calling. I find it written in the Bible, that " if any man will not work, neither shall he eat." (2 Thess. iii. 10.) Idleness was one of the sins of Sodom. Religion must be no pretence for slothfulness. Instead of giving up your worldly occupations, let it be your endeavour to carry them on in a Christian spirit. *Use* this world; but do not *abuse* it. Use it for God. Look upon it as a wilderness on your way to the promised Canaan; as the mariner regards the sea, not as a dwelling-place, but as a passage to his desired port.

Or if you are a *Trades-person,* try and act on the gospel rule in all your transactions. Be strictly honest, even in the smallest matter; and let the world see that a high principle guides you, and that your religion does not consist in bare words, but that it runs through all the actions of your life.

Or if you are *a Servant,* let the powerful influence of grace shew itself in all you do. Be as careful of your master's interests as of your own; and seek to win his confidence by your evident desire always to act rightly. Be kind, cheerful, and obliging to your fellow-servants; and let it be clearly seen that yours is a religion which gives you joy and peace, and which produces a holy and consistent walk.

Or, again, if you are *a Person of rank and influence,* use these talents in your Master's service; lay them out for the good of your fellow-creatures, and for His glory.

In almost every station of life we must of necessity be often thrown in with persons of a worldly character, and engaged in matters of an entirely worldly nature. Much reason then have we to be watchful, and to pray earnestly that we may be enabled to let our light shine brightly in whatever circumstances we are placed.

It is not necessary to go out of the station in which God has placed you in order to serve Him. Joseph of Arimathea did not cease from being "an honourable counsellor," when he became a Christian. Neither did Cornelius, the Roman officer, feel it necessary to quit the service of his country, when he joined the ranks of Christ. But there was this marked change in each of them—the one became a *Christian* counsellor, and the other a *Christian* soldier. They acted thenceforth as religious men, with the fear of God before their eyes, and the love of God in their hearts. And does not St. Paul say, " Let every man abide in the same calling, wherein he was called ? " (1 Cor. vii. 20.) It is clearly then our duty to try and glorify God in our several stations, whatever they be, and to carry the spirit of a Christian with us into our daily life.

But perhaps you will feel that this is no easy matter. I know your difficulties, and how little able you are of yourself to meet them. But remember Him who said, "My grace is sufficient for thee; for my strength is made perfect in weakness." (2 Cor. xii. 9.) The charge of being singular will probably be brought against you. But if you are Christ's servant, this is no more than you may expect; for His people have always been "men wondered at."

In fact, the true Christian must needs be in many respects very different from other men. There is a broad line, as it were, which marks off the path of each. The servant of Christ must not fall in with the corrupt ways of a sinful world. The Word of God warns of this, when it says, "Be not conformed to this world, but be ye transformed by the renewing of your minds." (Rom. xii. 2.) To use a familiar phrase, you must not cut the coat of your profession according to the fashion of those around you. It is said of a certain great Courtier, that being once asked how he managed always to keep in favour amidst great changes, when at one time a Popish king, and at another time a Protestant king, was on the throne—he replied, that "he was not born a *stubborn oak*, but a *bending osier*." And shall this be your character? No; there must be no wavering about you, no bending this way or that way to suit your own interest. You must be fixed in your principles, and not be blown about by every gust of wind.

I would not have you *aim at singularity*, either in your manner or in your conduct. This often does harm, and brings religion into contempt. To be singular in little and *unimportant* things, as a rule, is wrong. But in *important* matters, where the soul's interests are at stake, a stand should be made; there should be a "coming out, and being separate," a determination not even to "touch the unclean thing." 2 Cor. vi. 7.

But there are some points connected with our intercourse with the world which are of vital importance. There are certain practices which the world sanctions, but which are *positively hurtful* to the Christian, *positively hateful* to God, and clearly sinful in His sight. These you must carefully avoid, if you would be a candidate for heaven: you must resolutely, and at once, set your face against them.

For instance, did you once indulge in those pleasures which are hurtful to the soul? Did you find delight in such pastimes as are to be met with in the Fair, or on the Race-course? These must be given up. Some will perhaps say to you, "Only partake of such amusements *moderately*, and they will do you no harm." But I am bound to tell you that they are evil, and must be *altogether shunned;* for "what fellowship hath righteousness with unrighteousness? and what communion hath light with darkness?" Such places can no longer be fit for you; such pleasures cannot be congenial to a Christian's spirit.

Were you once fond of dress? Did you seek to be admired? Was the praise of your fellow-men sweet to your taste? Such must no longer be your feelings. They are altogether unsuited to a changed and sanctified heart. They are *of the world*, and not *of God*. Were you once, not actually dishonest perhaps, but a little too sharp about a bargain? Such a character would now but ill become you. You must be just, straightforward, honest, and upright in all your dealings.

And here let me meet a question which often perplexes a beginner in the Christian life—"What ought I to give up? Is this or that thing lawful?" "Is it right to go here or there—to do this or that?" It is by no means easy to lay down one general rule to meet every case. Many things, not wrong in themselves, may be hurtful to particular persons. Other things again are lawful, but not expedient. The best rules I can lay down for you are these—

1. Consult your Bible, and see if God says anything there on the matter you are doubting about.

2. Ask God to direct every step you take, and to guide your judgment, so that you may see clearly what is the right course.

3. Go nowhere, where you cannot ask God to go with you. Engage in nothing, on which you cannot entreat His blessing. Do nothing, which is likely to unfit you afterwards for religious exercises.

4. Whenever you *doubt* about a thing being lawful, remember, it is the safer course to avoid it.

But, after all, we must bear this in mind, that it is much easier to talk about giving up the world than to carry the resolution into effect. Our attachment to it is not laid aside in a moment. When we think we have done with it, it appears in some fresh shape. Like a wounded serpent, that we have set our foot upon, it presently creeps in again, when we imagine that we have utterly cast it out. And if we do not take care, it will sting us yet, though it seems so harmless. It requires indeed much grace to enable us to overcome the love of the world. Oh that we could reach that height which St. Paul had attained, when he said, "The world is crucified unto me, and I unto the world." Gal. vi. 14.

Again and again, as the Christian journeys on, here one difficulty, and there another, besets his path. He would be glad indeed to have some clear rule to guide him in every case, and under every circumstance. But God gives us no such precise rules. He often calls upon us to consider each case by itself. We must take each particular emergency, and act as we believe to be best, and most in accordance with God's Word. "Every day (says a Christian writer) does the seaman on his voyage take his observations, that he may rightly direct his course. He compares his position with his charts. He considers the direction of the wind, and the set of the tide. And from all these together he judges how to steer his vessel. And is not this an image of our own condition? We cannot have a guide at our right hand to tell us exactly what we should do, and where we should go, and how we should act, in every particular instance. What is right for one may be wrong for another. Our duty is, to try and act as we believe God would have us act; and our comfort is, that if at the same time, we honestly 'commit our ways unto the Lord,' He will, according to His promise, ' direct our steps.'"

2. LOOSE AND UNGODLY FRIENDSHIPS too are very apt to prove hurtful to the inexperienced Christian. Here then is another danger to be guarded against. It is not merely the companionship of the depraved and profligate that will do you harm, but also of the trifling, the idle, and the vain. But you may find it somewhat difficult to get rid of such companions, if you are already encumbered with them. A little caution is required in doing this. You must not shake them off too roughly, or you may needlessly stir up their enmity against you, and against the cause you have at heart. And yet they can never be your close associates. Take great care then that you are not actuated by a spirit of pride, as though you would say, "Stand by thyself, come not near; I am holier than thou." (Isaiah lxv. 5.) Behave kindly, and gently, and tenderly, even to those whom you know to be wrong. Remember you were once wrong yourself, and on some points, doubtless, you are wrong still. You were once

just as blind as they are, and your heart was as hard and worldly as theirs. Therefore be considerate towards them, and use every means in your power to do them good, and to win them over.

Possibly you may be placed in such a position that you must needs mix with worldly, or even ungodly, persons. If so, pray that you may be kept faithful to your heavenly Master. And I believe that in such a case God will throw his shield around you, and protect you from harm. But this is altogether different from deliberately choosing such as your companions. For if you willingly keep up an intimacy with those who despise religion, your soul will suffer; you will, almost without knowing it, fall in with their ways; your hatred of sin will be deadened; your love for the Saviour will grow cold; and so, by slow, but sure degrees, you will at length become like those with whom you associate.

No, dear reader, you cannot touch the fire without being burnt. You cannot even occasionally sip an unwholesome mixture, without feeling the bad effects to your own health. "Evil communications corrupt good manners." "Enter not," says the wise king, "into the path of the wicked, and go not into the way of evil men. Avoid it, pass not by it; turn from it, and pass away." (Prov. iv. 14.) "O my soul, come not thou into their secret. Unto their assembly, mine honour, be not thou united." (Gen. xlix. 6.) And let me say this —if you have still a hankering after the company of the ungodly and the worldly-minded, then begin to suspect that your own heart cannot be right with God. You cannot have become "a new creature," or you would assuredly find the ways, and the language, and the spirit of ungodly persons to be distasteful to you.

Then take a decided course. Make a firm stand. Cost what it may, *the companionship of the wicked must be shunned.* You must neither let smooth words, nor taunting expressions, move you from the strait and narrow path.

3. Another danger which serves to deter some is PERSECUTION. This you are pretty sure to meet with in one shape or other. And this is a danger to be prepared for. Persecution is the portion of Christ's servants. It is what they must expect; for the word of God says, " All that will live godly in Christ Jesus

shall suffer persecution." (2 Tim. iii. 12.) "The servant is not greater than his lord; if they have persecuted me, they will also persecute you." John xv. 20.

If you meet with persecution, it will try your faith; it will, perhaps, make you flinch a little, and feel half-disposed to shrink back. A jeering look from some old companion, or a discouraging word from one who ought to help you on; coldness from those who have been always in the habit of showing you kindness; houses closed against you, where once you always met with a welcome reception; false accusations brought against you, and wrong motives laid to your charge—all this is hard to bear. It has been said, with truth, that many a brave man, who would not fear to stand at a cannon's mouth, has trembled before the sneer of his fellow-man.

So it is. Our poor feeble hearts are apt to quail before the scorn of man. But it will comfort us to remember that Jesus has borne it before us. The prophets, and apostles, and early Christians passed through far hotter trials than yours. And the same God who supported them can strengthen you, and carry you through unhurt.

It is said of John Huss, the Bohemian martyr, that when he was brought out to be burnt, they put on his head a crown of paper with painted devils on it. On seeing it, he said, " My Lord Jesus Christ, for my sake, wore a crown of thorns; why should not I, then, for His sake, wear this light crown, be it ever so ignominious ? Truly, I will do it, and that willingly." When it was set upon his head, some who stood by said, " Now, we commit thy soul to the devil." " But I," said Huss, lifting up his eyes towards heaven, " do commit my spirit into thy hands, O Lord Jesus Christ."

And how do *you* feel when you are reproached, scorned, derided, and crowned with ignominy, for Jesus' sake ? Oh try and feel as the disciples felt, when " they departed from the presence of the council, *rejoicing that they were counted worthy to suffer shame for his name.*" Acts v. 41.

It is most likely, I say, that you will have something to bear. But no matter, if it is for *Christ's sake.* The enemies of religion may taunt you—they may treat you with violence —but if they go ever so far, they cannot really hurt you. They may break the casket, but they cannot touch the jewel within. Let not their opposition then distress you. "Fear not them that kill the body, but after that have no more that they can do." In the hour of trial look up for strength, and it will be given you; and feel it an honour to suffer for your Master's sake.

It is certainly desirable to exercise prudence, as well as boldness. But never think that any amount of prudence will keep you clear of all opposition from an ungodly world. "Many winter blasts (says Archbishop Leighton) will meet you in the way of religion, if you keep straight to it. Suffering and war with the world is a part of the godly man's portion here, which seems hard; but take it altogether it is sweet. None in their wits will refuse that legacy entire,—'In the world ye shall have tribulation, but in me ye shall have peace.' (John xvi. 33.) This is the path to the kingdom; that which all the sons of God have gone in, even Christ, as that known word is, 'One Son without *sin*, but none without *suffering*.' Persecution meets the Christian in his first entry into the path of the kingdom, and goes along all the way. No sooner canst thou begin to seek the way to heaven, but the world will seek how to vex and molest thee, and make that way grievous."

Do not, however, *seek* persecution. To fly from it is wrong; for if you are ashamed of Christ, He will be ashamed of you. But it is equally wrong to court it, and to run into it needlessly. If, then, you are free from persecution, be very thankful. But if it is forced upon you, do not shrink from it; but bear it cheerfully and patiently, "rejoicing that you are counted worthy to suffer shame for His name." (Acts v. 41.) "Blessed are ye (says our Lord) when men shall revile you and persecute you, and shall say all manner of evil against you falsely for my sake: rejoice and be exceeding glad, for great is your reward in heaven." Matt. v. 11, 12.

Be very careful never to lose your temper when spoken against. Think of your Lord, who, "when He was reviled, reviled not again, but committed himself to Him that judgeth righteously." (1 Peter ii. 23.) Meekly, and if possible even cheerfully, bear the cross that is laid upon you. And if you thus repay harsh words and rough treatment with kindness and love, you will be glorifying God, and smoothing your own path. Who knows but that your

Christian conduct may win over your very persecutors? Or, at all events, may not the time come when those who have treated you scornfully shall see their error?

Before closing this subject, I cannot forbear adding a word about those persecutions which many *bring upon themselves* by their own inconsistencies and unguarded conduct. We should never forget that it is only to those who are persecuted *"for righteousness' sake,"* that a blessing is promised. (Matthew v. 10.) If, therefore, we are smarting from this sharp weapon, which the world is ever too ready to use against the Christian, will it not be well to look a little closely into the matter, and see whether we may not, in part at least, have drawn this evil upon ourselves. There may have been something in our conduct, our words, our manner of speaking, or in our general bearing, which has perhaps almost *invited* persecution. For instance, we may be a little sharp and censorious in our language; we may carry ourselves in an overbearing manner; we may have zeal without prudence. These and other causes may have given rise to the ill-treatment we have received, and which has caused us so much distress. Surely we shall do well to take our daily conduct seriously to task, in order to discover, and cast out, whatever may be causing needless offence.

Happy for us, if no blame lies at our own door. " Rejoice (says the Apostle) inasmuch as ye are partakers of Christ's sufferings, that when his glory shall be revealed, ye may be glad also with exceeding joy."

The following was the prayer of one of our own persecuted Bishops, who died as a martyr for the truth of Christ:—" The Lord grant us his heavenly grace and strength, that we may confess Him in the world, amongst this adulterous and sinful generation; that He may confess us at the latter day before his Father which is in heaven, to his glory, and our everlasting comfort, joy, and salvation."—*Bishop Ridley.*

CHAPTER IX.

DANGERS FROM WITHIN.

AN EVIL HEART.—PRIDE.—TEMPER.—UNCHARITABLE-NESS.—SELFISHNESS.—IDLENESS.—INFLUENCE OF BAD HABITS.

THE Christian is now in an enemy's country. He is living in a world at enmity for the most part against his Lord, and against himself as one of His followers. He is exposed, therefore, as we have seen, to numberless *outward Dangers*. But these are not all; nor indeed are they his worst enemies. Besides these, there are *Dangers from within*—enemies in the very citadel of his own heart. I shall now speak of these. And may God speak by me for your profit!

To begin with, I would have you always bear this in mind—that we have all of us

AN EVIL HEART.

to contend with *a corrupt and evil heart.* Although the heart may have been renewed by the Holy Spirit, there is a remnant of sin and corruption, which still clings to us, and will cling to us to the very last. Hence, in every really earnest soul there is a continual and mighty struggle: "the old man" rebels against "the new man." There is an inward conflict ever going on. All God's people feel this more or less. Hear what St. Paul says of himself; "To will is present with me; but how to perform that which is good I find not; for the evil that I would not, that I do." " I find then a law, that when I would do good evil is present with me." Rom. vii.

In the beginning of a Christian's course, he is often disposed to fancy that the work of grace is already completed, that the warfare is over, and that henceforth all will be smooth and peaceful. And then he thinks it strange to find himself tried and perplexed by inward struggles. He believes; and fancies that he shall never again be troubled by weakness of faith. The flame of love burns brightly in his heart; and he imagines that it will never flag, or grow dim again. Ah, but he forgets that he has within him this *evil heart*, always ready to go wrong. For, though he can say with thankfulness, "I delight in the law of God, after the inward man," he is forced, by sad experience, to add, "But I see *another law* in my members *warring against the law of my mind,* and leading me into captivity to the law of sin which is in my members." Rom. vii. 22, 23.

Marvel not, then, dear Christian reader, if you find that there is a sore conflict going on within you. But rather rejoice; for it is a proof that there is life in your soul. Neither marvel, if you feel the weight and pressure of indwelling sin; for the more you know of true holiness, the more sensible will you be of the existence of sin within you, and the more you will be distressed at its presence. How was it that, time back, you felt nothing of all this? There were no "fightings within" then; no strivings for the mastery; no groanings for deliverance. No; for Satan at that time held you fast. Your soul was slumbering; it was "sleeping the sleep of death."

Be thankful if it is otherwise with you now. And be not surprised when I tell you, that you will have to carry on a vigorous and unceasing warfare against the corruptions of your own heart, as long as you remain here.

Let me now try and point out to you in what various ways these corruptions will shew themselves. And so let me put you upon your guard.

1. Beware of PRIDE. But you will say, perhaps, "Now that I have taken the gospel as my rule, is there any fear of pride springing up in my heart?" Yes, there is much fear of it. There is a root of Pride *naturally* growing in every heart. And this shews itself even in God's people. Poor foolish man is pleased with being made much of. He likes to feel that he is of some consequence. The idea of being looked down upon, and passed by, is very painful to most of us. We can bear anything sooner than this. Many of us would be willing, if called upon, to undergo actual suffering for Christ's sake. We could endure persecution. All this is much easier than to put up with contempt, and to be little esteemed by those about us. And yet cheerfully to accept this is Christ-like. This is what He bore so willingly for us; and it is what we should be willing to bear also. Such is the true spirit of the gospel—not merely to *confess* that we are nothing, but to *feel* that we

are nothing, and to be willing that *others should think so too*—to feel no repining at being overlooked, cast into the shade, yea, trampled under foot. Oh, what an attainment is this! And yet how few, how very few, reach it!

But there is also such a thing as **spiritual** pride. And this is an evil into which many a young believer falls. Now that the Holy Spirit has begun to enlighten you, and you already see things, as it were, with new eyes, and know many truths which you were, but a short time ago, quite ignorant of, perhaps you feel astonished that others can be so blind. Then comes the Tempter, and fills you with the notion that you are better than they, that your sight is clearer, your knowledge greater, and your strength firmer. You are also tempted perhaps to feel that you are on a rock, and fancy that you shall never be moved.

If it be so with you, let me put in a word in time. You see more than you once did, and more perhaps than many; but there is much dimness yet. You have much still to learn. Your strength is only weakness. Can that little infant, which you notice in the street, walk alone? It may try; but it will fall. Its mother's hand must lead it, and its mother's arm support it. And *you* are but as a little child. The " everlasting arms " must be underneath you, or your strength will surely give way. " Let him that thinketh he standeth take heed lest he fall."

The holiest men are generally the humblest. Was Abraham proud? He speaks of himself as "dust and ashes." (Gen. xviii. 27.) Was Isaiah proud? He says, " I am a man of unclean lips." (Is. vi. 5.) Was Jeremiah proud? When God called him to his high office, his answer shows how unworthy he felt himself of so great an honour; "Ah, Lord God, behold, I cannot speak, for I am a child." (Jer. i. 6.) Was St. Paul proud? He felt himself to be " less than the least of all saints ; " "not meet to be called an apostle." Eph. iii. 8 ; 1 Cor. xv. 9.

But, observe here, there is such a thing as *false* humility, which, in fact, is nothing more nor less than pride in its very worst shape. When, for instance, a man speaks of himself as being nothing, in order that he may get the credit of being *thought humble ;* or when he is for ever *talking* of his sinfulness, and yet has no sorrow on account of sin—this is nothing but a dressed-up humility. It is pride, under another name; and if it lurks in your breast, may God strip you, and take it from you!

It is not a humble *appearance* merely that we want, or a humble *speech*, or a humble *character* among men, but a *humble heart*, and a *humble walk*. Oh that we may be sincere in this matter! Oh that we may be low in our own eyes, and willing to be low in the eyes of others!

There is a great charm in Humility. Even the world knows something of its loveliness. But, what is of more consequence, it is pleasing in the sight of God: "He hath respect unto the lowly, but the proud He knoweth afar off." (Ps. cxxxviii. 6.) It is "the poor in spirit" that He loves to "satisfy with good things." And it is "to the humble" that "He giveth more grace." "His sweet dews and showers of grace (says Archbishop Leighton) slide off the mountains of pride, and fall on the low valleys of humble hearts, and make them pleasant and fertile." Another Christian writer remarks, that "the emptier the vessel, and the lower it is let down in the well, the more water it draws up; so the more the soul is emptied of self, and the lower it is let down by humility, the more it fetcheth out of the well of salvation." The bough that bears the most fruit usually bends the lowest.

Seek, then, a really humble, lowly, meek spirit. Think much of God's greatness and holiness, and then look at your own littleness and vileness. Ask the Lord to lift up the veil, and constantly shew you to yourself. Ask Him to keep you daily from pride. Learn to "walk humbly with thy God;" for, as has been well said, " He who walks humbly cannot fall, since he is down already." Remember, too, that it is written, "Pride goeth before destruction." Bend thy neck to the Saviour's gentle yoke. Go with Mary, and sit at the feet of Jesus, and "learn of Him, for He was meek and lowly in heart."

How sweet, and how true, are the words of the Christian poet on this point :—

"The bird that soars on highest wing
    Builds on the ground her lowly nest;
And she that doth most sweetly sing
    Sings in the shade, when all things rest.
In lark and nightingale we see
What honour hath humility.

"When Mary chose the better part,
   She meekly sat at Jesus' feet ;
And Lydia's gently-opened heart
   Was made for God's own temple meet.
Fairest and best adorned is she
Whose clothing is humility.

"The saint that wears heaven's brightest crown
   In deepest adoration bends;
The weight of glory bows him down
   Then most, when most his soul ascends.
Nearest the throne itself must be
The footstool of humility."

The process by which God teaches us humility is sometimes a most painful one. It must be so. For the cutting down and crushing of pride is a severe work. There are hours when the soul of the believer is made to smart bitterly. But when he is thus taken down into the valley of humiliation much salutary truth is learnt, which would not otherwise come home to the heart. Grace abounds in that valley; and he comes out of it more lowly, but more happy—more distrustful of himself, but more full of confidence, as he looks out of himself to his God.

2. EVIL TEMPER is another form in which

the corruption of our hearts will break out. Disliking to be contradicted, hastiness and impatience with those about us, moroseness and sullenness—all these are so many symptoms of that disease which lurks in our fallen nature. But it is quite impossible for us to enjoy happiness, as long as they remain uncurbed.

There are few things which make a man more thoroughly wretched than an unruly temper. He becomes a perfect misery, both to himself, and to those who are living with him. And, of course, while this is the case God's work of grace cannot be prospering in his soul. He may love to hear the truth, and he may wish to follow it; but no sooner does he take a step in advance than some fit of unconquered temper throws him back; and he immediately feels that he has sinned against God, and separated himself from Him.

We often hear a person say, " My temper is naturally bad;" as if this was a sufficient excuse for giving way to sin. We are apt to lay as much blame upon *nature* as we can. It is true that some are born more amiable and gentle than others. But, certainly, no one has a temper so naturally good that it needs no subduing, or a temper so naturally bad that it cannot, by God's grace, be restrained.

You are sometimes discouraged, it may be, in your attempt to correct a quick, irritable, and bad temper. But no: make it a matter of conscience; look upon it as a part of the great daily work you have to do; and never rest till it is accomplished. Entreat God to help you; and you will in the end gain the victory. No doubt you will have many a hard fight, but success will be sure to follow the endeavour. You have this precious promise to encourage you: " Sin shall not *have dominion over you:* for ye are not under the law, but under grace." Rom. vi. 14.

Begin, then, in earnest, if you have not begun already. And never give up the struggle, till you have mastered this enemy. Think not, however, to overcome in your own unassisted strength, but by God's help, and by the power of his Holy Spirit. *Determine* to conquer this evil; for it is hateful in any one, but peculiarly hateful in a child of God. He, of all men, should be loving, and gentle, and forbearing. He should " suffer long, and be kind." And it should be seen that grace has softened his *temper,* as well as his *heart.*

Now, is there any one point in which your temper is wont to show itself? Is there any one thing which tries you more than another?

Does your Parent require something of you which you may think a little unnecessary, and does a feeling of sullenness or of impatience spring up within you? Or does the waywardness of your Child irritate you? Or, does the conduct of your Neighbour vex you? Or the unreasonableness of your Master or Mistress? Or the disobedience of your Servant? Take that one particular temptation, whatever it may be, and in God's strength try to get the mastery over it. If you succeed, how happy will you be! You will have an immediate reward. For is there not an inward pleasure in having done that which a Christian ought to do? Is there not happiness in the thought, that you have checked some wrong feeling, that was just ready to spring up within you—that you have hushed some storm that was on the very point of bursting forth? Is there not a peculiar happiness in feeling that those little things, which used to irritate you, now glide by, and leave you unharmed? Truly this is gaining what the Word of God declares to be the greatest of victories—" He that is slow to anger is better than the mighty; and *he that ruleth his spirit* than he that taketh a city." Proverbs xvi. 32.

It is said of the famous astronomer, Sir Isaac Newton, that he had a favourite little dog, named Diamond. Being one evening called out of his study into the next room, Diamond was left behind. When Sir Isaac returned, having been absent but a few minutes, he had the mortification to find that Diamond had overturned a lighted candle among some papers which had cost him many years' labour. The papers were in flames, and almost reduced to ashes. This loss, especially at Newton's great age, was irreparable. But, without at all punishing the dog, he merely exclaimed, "O Diamond, Diamond, you little know the mischief you have done."

Reader, what would *you* have done in these circumstances? The great Newton was *above* losing his temper. Are you above this frailty? Let nothing rob you of your self-control. Let the peace of God be ever ruling within you, "keeping your heart and mind," and preserving you calm and unruffled even under the most trying circumstances.

3. Another dangerous fault which often makes its appearance, especially in young converts, is UNCHARITABLENESS. A person, who

has only lately been awakened, is very apt to judge a little severely and to speak a little harshly, of those who do not think and feel just as he does. He seems to forget the condition that he himself was so lately in. And although he knows himself to be a monument of God's marvellous patience, he is himself impatient towards his brethren.

Can this be right! It is sad, indeed, to hear a Christian speaking against his neighbour, and taking upon himself to find fault with this or that point in his character. It plainly shows that he knows but little of his own heart; or else he would surely be more tender of a brother, and more ready to condemn himself.

It has been observed that, there are some men who are always looking on the dark side of people's character; so that one glaring fault, or even a single failing, will eclipse in their eyes a thousand excellences. Such persons are for ever complaining that religion makes no progress; for they can see nobody around them who is perfect; and therefore they come to the conclusion that there is very little piety in the world. They are disposed to take a gloomy view of everything, and to speak against everybody.

Now, if we find ourselves indulging in such a spirit, it is a plain proof that we have but little of the mind of Christ, and that we have much yet to learn. For you may be sure of this—that where a person is disposed to think harshly and unkindly of others, he probably knows but very little of his own heart.

To you, then, my reader, I would say—whenever you find yourself about to indulge in uncharitable remarks on your neighbour, whether a professing Christian or otherwise, just stop yourself, and say, " Let me have a peep at my own heart first." Be very careful to avoid this fault. It is a hateful one to fall into, and even the world condemns it. May we not ourselves have some grievous failings, which are hidden even from our nearest friends, and which are known only to God? And if these were brought out to light, would they not condemn *us?* Oh, then, let us deal very tenderly with our brother, and make every allowance for him. It is better, far better, to be as the Lark that is ever rising upwards, and hovers wistfully over her own little nest, than as the quick-eyed Eagle, which pounces so eagerly on its prey.

Let us take this for a rule—and a golden rule it is—to speak but little of *others*, and but little of *ourselves;* and also to be very backward in saying anything of a neighbour, unless we have *something good* to say of him. Let the world, if it will, be open-mouthed in its harsh judgments. Let it be eagle-eyed in discovering faults and blemishes in others. But let *us* be anxious to look at home—remembering that good man's resolution who said, that " whenever he spied a fault in his neighbour, he was determined to look for two in himself"— remembering also our Lord's precepts ; " Judge not, that ye be not judged ; " " First cast out the beam *out of thine own eye*, and then shalt thou see clearly to cast out the mote out of thy brother's eye." (Matt. vii. 1, 5.) Let us seek to have much of that Christian charity, or love, which " covereth a multitude of sins,"— that is, which delights rather to cloak them over, than to expose them to view. If such is our spirit, we shall I am sure be much happier and more useful, and we shall much more "adorn the doctrine of God our Saviour."

I have often thought, that it would be well if every Christian made it a rule to read over, two or three times in every year, that beautiful lesson on Christian charity which is contained in 1 Cor. xiii.

4. SELFISHNESS is another evil root, which grows naturally in the soil of man's heart, and chokes the beautiful seeds of grace as they spring up. Of this too the heart must be cleared.

"Every man for himself," is a maxim which we hear very commonly from the lips of worldly men. But how utterly opposed is this to the spirit of the Gospel! There we are taught the very opposite principle—"Let no man seek his own, but every man another's wealth," or welfare. (1 Cor. x. 24.) The Christian should live no longer to himself, but unto Him who redeemed him. He has been "bought with a price;" and therefore he is no longer his own, but God's. He should lay himself out for the glory of God, and for the good of his fellow-creatures. He should be *un*selfish.

How blest will your life be, if thus spent— not seeking merely *your own* happiness, but trying to make *others* happy, and to do *others* good—not selfishly asking, "How can I secure my own interests in the world?" but "How can I live to God?" "What can I do for

Him?" "How can I add to the happiness of my neighbour, my friend, or my brother?" Oh, this is blessedness indeed! An unselfish spirit has its own reward. The feeling that we are denying ourselves for the sake of others —the hope that by a little effort we may be of use to our brethren—the yielding up of something that we may have set our hearts upon, in order that we may do some act of kindness to a neighbour or a friend, is in itself delightful. It may cost us something; but who can tell what a plentiful harvest of joy the heart is sure to gather by it? " Look not every man on his own things, but every man also on the things of others." (Phil. ii. 4.) This was the Apostle's rule, and let it be *your* rule likewise. Ask yourself, if there is any one of your fellow-creatures, to whom you may be spiritually useful; or any one in want, whom you may relieve; or in distress, whom you may comfort. And though you may be in very humble circumstances, there are many ways in which you may be doing good. Only beg of God to give you the heart to feel, and the will to act, and you may be a real blessing to many. It may be said of Unselfishness, as it has been said of Mercy, "It is twice blest: it blesseth him that gives, and him that takes."

5. About IDLENESS I have a few words to say. The Christian should be active and diligent. There is a great work to be done for *God*, and for *your soul;* and if you would do it, there is no time to be lost. Sin is to be overcome. An evil nature is to be subdued. Holiness is to be attained. Heaven is to be won. Then be earnest in the matter. "The kingdom of heaven suffereth violence, and *the violent* (that is, *the earnest*) take it by force." (Matt. xi. 12.) Too many of our days have been frittered away; then let us "redeem the time" that yet remains. Was St. Paul idle? Let him speak for himself: "This *one thing* I do, forgetting those things which are behind, and reaching forth unto those things which are before, *I press toward the mark.*" Phil. iii. 13, 14.

One likes to see a Christian man earnest too *even in his worldly calling.* Is he a Magistrate? Let him be an active magistrate. Is he a Farmer? Let him not allow the weeds to grow under his feet. Is he engaged in any business? Let him undertake it heartily.

Is he a Servant? Let him be an active, diligent, and faithful servant. Is he a Labourer? Let him be an industrious labourer, not working merely when the master's eye is upon him, but when no one sees him but God. Whatever he takes up should be accomplished with zeal. It should be done heartily, and it should be done well. " Whatsoever (says Solomon) thy hand findeth to do, *do it with thy might.*" (Eccl. ix. 10.) It is said of King Hezekiah, that " in every work that he began in the service of the house of God, and in the law, and in the commandments, to seek his God, he did it *with his whole heart.*" 2 Chron. xxxi. 21.

We should be very watchful about *wasting time.* Our time is more valuable to us even than our money; for, when once gone, it cannot be recovered. Good old Mr. Alleine used to say, " Give me a Christian who counts his time more precious than gold." And Seneca, the Heathen, teaches us that " Time is the only thing of which it is a virtue to be covetous." Are you making the most of it? Are you laying it out for God? Are you spending every moment, as one who must give an account? Are you gathering up every fragment of time, that nothing be lost? Are you like the goldsmith, who all the year long saves the very sweepings of his shop, because it may contain filings of some precious metal? How much, in this respect, may be gained by a little arrangement! Just as we see some thrifty persons making a few shillings go as far as others can make as many pounds go; so it is with our time: by a careful husbanding of it we may do great things.

But remember, you may waste your time, and yet be busy. There is such a thing as *a busy idleness.* You may seem to be actively engaged; and yet, in fact, be doing nothing all the while. You may be employing yourself about the veriest trifles; and all the while be neglecting matters of great importance. You may be busy about the world; and yet be leaving the things of God undone. Happy those who are ever acting upon the Apostle's motto, "Not slothful in business, fervent in spirit, serving the Lord."

Here I must throw in a word about *Early Rising.* I look upon this almost as a Christian duty; at least, where there is no impediment in the way. I am persuaded that it tends not a little to our bodily and spiritual health, our comfort, and our usefulness. That hour which is redeemed from unnecessary sleep, in the very prime of the day, is far more precious than any other. No time is so valuable for devotion; and at no hour is the mind more alert for any active employment.

Make up your mind, dear reader, to be an *Early Riser;* you will soon find that you are abundantly repaid for any little effort it may cost you.

And this will help you to cultivate another habit—that of *Punctuality.* Let it be a matter of conscience with you never to be late for anything, and never to act as one in a hurry. It was said of an eminent Christian minister that his mind was so well regulated, that, although his engagements were often numerous and pressing, he never seemed to be hurried, but always calm, and that this could be traced even in so small a matter as his handwriting. Everything he did was done quietly, and without bustle.

Let such regularity and order shew itself in all you do. If you have an engagement with a neighbour for a certain hour, be at your post at that hour; otherwise you may be robbing him of the time he can ill spare, as well as disturbing your own plans. Or, if you have a duty to perform, do not put it off, but let it be discharged without delay. Or, if you have a payment to make, let it be made, if possible, at the time fixed.

Make something of a plan for each day; and accustom yourself to look forward a little to see that the way will be clear for any appointed engagement. Be regular in the disposal of your time. Be careful of *moments*. Let every part of the day have its *allotted* employment. Always have some *useful* work in hand.

It is *possible* however for a methodical person to carry his rules too far; when, for instance, he becomes irritable, if his regular habits are at all broken in upon; or when he is vexed, if others are not as orderly as himself. Plans and rules are excellent things,—but, as has been well said, " they should be made of *leather*, not of *stone*."

It is in these little things, as well as in great things, that the Christian's character shines forth; and by them it is plainly seen that he desires to do *all* to God's glory.

I cannot finish this chapter without observing

that any *Bad Habits* which we may have once formed will, if let alone, prove to be great impediments to us in our Christian career. They have been allowed perhaps to grow up with our growth, and have almost become part of ourselves. And now that we desire to follow Christ, they are still ready to cling to us, and we find it hard, very hard, to shake them off.

This is indeed a sore let and hindrance to us in our spiritual race. "Suppose you were compelled to wear an iron collar about your neck through life, or a chain upon your ankle, would it not be a burden every day and hour of your existence? You would rise in the morning a prisoner to your chain; you would lie down at night weary with your burden; and you would groan the more deeply, as you reflected there was no shaking it off."

And is it less miserable to be tied, and bound, and hampered by some bad habit which clogs us and keeps us back, when we would be going forward? If you feel this, oh! lose not a moment in trying to disencumber yourself. Be constantly making war against that habit, whatever it be.

And here, since the heart is so treacherous and deceitful that it will often shelter itself under a willing ignorance of what its besetting sins and dangers may be, let me name a few bad habits, by one or more of which it is possible you may be entangled, leaving it to your own conscience to make the application:—

A habit of wasting time in idle gossip;

A habit of listlessness when reading God's word;

A habit of slothfulness, and indulgence in sleep, and so hurrying over the morning devotions;

A habit of putting off what ought to be done at the moment;

A habit of disputing and contradicting;

A habit of exaggerating and colouring reports when you repeat them;

A habit of allowing your eyes and thoughts to wander when in the house of God;

A habit of peevish fretfulness, when you ought to be contented and thankful;

A habit of "building castles in the air;"

A habit of spying out the faults and imperfections of others.

Here, then, I have mentioned a few Bad Habits; others will readily occur to you. Perhaps some one of them may have long proved a snare to you. It may cling very tightly, and you may fancy that it is almost impossible to shake it off. But if you would grow in grace, it *must* be parted with. That sin, though it be but a little one, will hinder you in your course. Your usefulness is marred by it. Your advance is checked by it. It is true, you can never release yourself, if you rely upon your own power. But God will supply you with strength, in answer to your earnest prayer. And He will make you to feel in your own case the truth of those words, "I can do *all things* through Christ who strengtheneth me." Phil. iv. 13.

Now, try this. It is more than likely you are suffering from some bad habit. Bring that, whatever it be, before God. Tell Him that it greatly troubles you, and that you earnestly desire to master it. Ask Him to give you special help for this special purpose. Only make the trial; and I am sure you will find this one of the great secrets of growth in grace.

CHAPTER X.

TEMPTATIONS OF SATAN.

MANY of the dangers mentioned in the last chapter arise from the actual assaults of Satan, of which I am now going to speak more especially. It is often difficult to distinguish between a direct temptation of *the Devil* and the natural inclinations of *our own evil hearts.* The fact is that the two usually work together. Our wicked hearts desire a thing that is sinful; and then Satan, who carefully studies the heart, takes advantage of us, and thrusts sin in our way. We lay ourselves open; and then he attacks us. The soil is prepared by ourselves; and then he casts in the evil seed. If we were sinless beings, his temptations would be all in vain; they would fly over us, and we should be unhurt. But we are naturally disposed to what is evil. Our hearts are like a fire, in which the spark of sin is smouldering, and the Evil Spirit is ever blowing up the flame within us. Temptation first finds a man corrupt, and then makes him worse. For, alas, there is not one among us who can say, as our sinless Lord said, "The Prince of this world cometh, and hath nothing in me."

That there is such a being as Satan is very clear from Scripture, even if our own experience did not tell us so. He is there described as a Fallen Angel, an Evil Spirit, who is ever employed in plotting and planning our spiritual ruin. He is spoken of as tempting Adam and Eve in Paradise (Gen. iii.); as provoking David to sin against the Lord, by numbering Israel (1 Chron. xxi. 1); as trying to make Job rebel against God (Job i. 11; ii. 5); as entering into the heart of the traitor Judas, and leading him to become the betrayer of his heavenly Master (Luke xxii. 3); as filling the heart of Ananias, and inducing him to lie against the Holy Ghost. Acts v. 3.

And, most assuredly, he will attack *you;* for *now* he makes more efforts than ever to ruin your soul. When you were asleep he cared not to arouse you. He then let you alone. "The strong man armed" kept the palace, and "the goods were in peace." All was as he would have it. He was quite satisfied with your condition. But now, if he sees that through God's mercy you are awake, and anxious to be saved, he will leave no means untried to draw your soul away from God.

I put you then upon your guard. "Be vigilant (or watchful); because your adversary the devil, as a roaring lion, walketh about seeking whom he may devour." (1 Pet. v. 8.) Expect his temptations. Be always on the look-out for them. They will come to you in ten thousand shapes.

For instance, he tempts one man by riches, and another by poverty. He suggests to one man hard thoughts of God; another he puffs up with self-esteem. Sometimes he entices us openly; at other times secretly. He attacks one man when alone; a second he tempts when in company; a third upon his knees; a fourth whilst reading the word of God, or even in the house of God. Thus he suits his temptations to our several cases. He knows that what will be a temptation to one man, will be no temptation to another; and that what would be a strong temptation at one time, will be utterly powerless at another time.

In your case, for example, he is quite aware that the temptation, which took effect upon you a while ago, would very likely fall harmless upon you now. So he changes it. Perhaps he *once* tried to persuade you that it was *too soon* to repent—that there was time enough yet. *Now*, it may be, he throws in the thought that your repentance is *too late*. He formerly led you to hope that all would come right at last, though you were then living without God. And now he harasses you at times with the feeling that there is no hope for you, though you earnestly desire to be saved.

There are peculiar temptations, too, which beset each person. Into some you are much more liable to fall than into others. Some will meet you in one place, and some in another; some in one shape, and some in another. It is very important to know *where* you are most exposed to temptation, and at those points to set a strong and watchful guard.

With regard to temptation generally, it may be observed, that it is better to avoid it than to face it. A writer on this subject remarks: " At some particular time of the day, or in some particular situations, you find yourself exposed to debasing and corrupting thoughts. They fill your mind, and crowd out everything that is good. These temptations arise only when you are alone, or when you are conversing on some particular subjects, or when something is recalled by the memory. Can you hope to conquer these 'legions,' and drive away all these 'unclean birds,' by any other means than *by fleeing from them?* As there are some evil spirits, which, it is said, cannot be cast out except 'by prayer and fasting,' so these can be overcome only by avoiding and resisting them, *when they approach the heart;* or by the most sincere prayer, *when they have entered it.* If Peter be naturally impetuous, ought he not to leave his sword behind him? Should Judas carry the bag, when he has fully proved to himself that he cannot do it without stealing from it? Should a passionate man, whose temper is easily excited, throw himself into situations in which he will certainly be tempted to anger? Whatever be your weakness, or the spot at which you fall, beware of it, and shun it."

You see then in how many ways our great enemy attacks us. He is strong; but, thank God, there is One stronger. He can *tempt* us to sin; but he cannot *force* us to sin. And when we consider the violence and subtlety of his temptations, what an unspeakable mercy it is, that he can do no more than *tempt* us! We are weak and powerless in ourselves; but God stands ever ready to strengthen and uphold us. And if we commit ourselves to Him, "He will, with the temptation, also make a way to escape." 1 Cor. x. 13.

And, oh, how often does He, our ever-watchful Guardian, shelter us without our knowing it! Satan has, perhaps, spread his net for us, and has, as it were, made it of so curious and fine a thread, as not to be seen by our eye: and so we go hasting on towards our ruin. But suddenly the mercy of God's providence stops us in our course, and pulls back our foot from the fatal snare.

Truly we are secure, only so long as we are in God's safe keeping. If we have not entrusted ourselves to Him, then are we like a ship sailing without a pilot, amidst hidden rocks; and we may at any moment be wrecked.

The Lord gives us, in James iv. 7, both a *Command* which shows us what our duty is, and also a *Promise* to encourage us,—"Resist the devil, and he will flee from you."

The *Command* of God, you see, is, "Resist

the devil." And it is your wisdom to set about obeying this command. To tempt is the devil's work: to resist is the Christian's duty.

It is very important to *resist the first motions of evil*. When a temptation comes, look up to God instantly for strength; if you parley with the tempter, you are lost. Mark carefully the steps by which Eve was ensnared. First, *she stood near* the forbidden tree. Then, when Satan proposed to her to eat of it, *she argued with him*. Then *she looked at the fruit*, and " saw that it was good for food, and pleasant to the eyes." The temptation gained upon her, and she presently *touched it*. And at last she finished by *eating it*. St. Paul charges us not to "give place to the devil." Oh, let us not yield a single point to him. We know that a beggar, who may seem to be very modest out of doors, will, if once let in, command the house. And so, if we yield only a little to the tempter at first, we are in fact giving away our strength, and shall have the less to resist him afterwards. "When the hem is torn, the whole garment is nearly sure to ravel out."

It has been said of the Cuckoo, that she enters the sparrow's nest, and there lays her egg. And the poor little owner unconsciously warms it into life, to the destruction of her own brood, which the usurper in the end thrusts out of the nest. So a temptation may be allowed to nestle in the heart for a time, undisturbed and unfeared, until it ends by thrusting out all peace, and joy, and comfort, from the soul.

Now, if you would keep the devil out of your life and actions, you must keep him first out of your thoughts and desires; for that is where he commonly begins to enter. If you would conquer sin, you must nip it in the bud, and not wait till it is fully formed within you. Have you not sometimes suffered your thoughts to dwell on some sinful object, and to brood upon it with delight, picturing it to yourself under its most pleasing forms? This is *most dangerous*. When a temptation gets thus far, it rarely happens that it is stopped. Hear what the wise Apostle says;—" Every man is tempted, when he is drawn away of his own lust and enticed. Then, when lust hath conceived, it bringeth forth sin; and sin, when it is finished, bringeth forth death." (James i. 14, 15.) You are tempted to sin, and you are quite resolved not to be led into it. But you, perhaps, like to please yourself a little while with the thought. You have no intention of actually committing the sin; but you think that you may play with it a little, as it were, and yet remain unhurt. And what is the consequence? It either ends in your committing the sin, or else your soul is injured by the nearness of it: it becomes weakened and unstrung; God is driven away; and your peace is gone.

Oh, how long does the effect of one single act of sin stand by us! The sin may be put away, but, like the snail, it leaves a slimy track behind it. When the Israelites had worshipped the golden calf, and so offended God, Moses prayed for them, and they were spared. But they did not go altogether unpunished. It was a common saying ever after, among the Jewish writers, that never did any judgment befal the children of Israel from that time forward, but "there was an ounce of the golden calf in it."

Remember also that many of those temptations, which *do not appear to be very hurtful*, are frequently the most dangerous. Satan very often puts a gloss upon sin, and makes it look fair; for we are told that he will, sometimes, if it suits his purpose, "transform himself into an angel of light." (2 Cor. xi. 14.) And then, at other times, he will try to conceal from us the greatness of a sin. He whispers in our ear, "Spare it; it is but a little one." And so we slight and trifle with the temptation, and think but lightly of it, because we are not really persuaded that there can be much evil at the bottom of that which looks so fair at top. Or, if this will not do, he will appear only to desire that its execution may be stayed awhile, as Jephthah's daughter, when she said, "Let me alone a month or two, and then do to me according to that which hath proceeded out of thy mouth"—well knowing that such reprieved sins at last obtain their full liberty.

Or, he will set things before you, which are *not sinful in themselves*, but which *lead to sin*. He will draw you into some pleasant path, as it were, where you may see nothing to alarm you, where you may even find some things that are good. But he will gently and gradually lead you on, till he has brought you, without knowing it, to the very edge of the pit of destruction.

Again, if he finds you fond of any particular occupation, which in itself is not only harmless, but even desirable, he will endeavour to make you give up your whole heart to it.

In short, any expedient will he resort to, in order to draw away your mind from the great object of life. I mention this to put you on your guard.

Let me now counsel you on another point—it is to avoid *disputed and doubtful questions*. The devil often endeavours to entrap and perplex the thoughtful with this snare. When he sees them concerned about their souls, and interested in religion, he confuses them in this way, and so draws off their attention from the all-important matter. Do not, if you can possibly avoid it, have anything to do with curious questions which " do gender strifes." But be content to dwell chiefly on those great and simple truths, which concern your salvation.

Gurnal, from whom I have taken more than one idea in this chapter, calls this "*keeping the plains.*" And so long as we do this, we are safe. When one army attacks another, they often try to get the enemy hemmed in between hills, or in some ground where they are at a disadvantage. Thus the Egyptians were hoping to say of their enemies, the Israelites, " They are entangled in the land; the wilderness hath shut them in." Exod. xiv. 3.

'And so your enemy will seek to entangle

you. He will lead you, if possible, to dwell upon difficult texts and hard passages of Scripture. He will get you to discuss disputed points of doctrine, to argue about Calvinism, and Arminianism, or about some disputed Church question; and so, if he possibly can, he will call off your attention from those matters, which more deeply concern the salvation of your soul. But, if you are wise, you will *keep to the plains*.

Again, serious persons sometimes puzzle themselves to find a reason for God's particular dealings with them. They want to discover a *why* and a *wherefore* for all He does. But no; if you are His child, you must be content with what your Father allots; and what you "know not now," you shall "know hereafter." Let me again remind you of Gurnal's advice— "*Keep to the plains.*" Do not try to dive into mysteries. "The *secret things* belong unto the Lord; but *those things which are revealed* belong unto us and to our children." Deut. xxix. 29.

Time back, when you were very young, did not your *Parents* bid you do many things, without giving you their reasons for the command? You could not *then* understand why they would have you do this, or abstain from that. But your duty was clear—simply to obey their directions, though you had no idea *why* they were given. And so should it be with regard to *God's* dealings with you. It matters little to know *why* He acts in this or that way towards you: it is your duty and your happiness, simply and without a murmur, to bow to His almighty will.

But of all temptations, none is more dreadful than when Satan tempts us with *unbelieving*, and even *sceptical, thoughts*. And in this way he does sometimes attack God's children. Yes, my dear Christian reader, he may by this particular temptation assault you. You may be tempted to doubt whether the Scripture is the word of God, and whether Christ is the Son of God, and whether there be a heaven or a hell. This temptation is very likely to prevail with persons of an inquisitive mind, and who are unsettled in the faith; and still more with those who have only a head knowledge of the gospel. But any one who has received God's word "in the love of it," and has *tasted* it as the very food of his soul, will be so persuaded of its preciousness, that nothing will shake his faith in it. He will "have the witness in himself." Suppose a minister were to tell his congregation that in some distant country there was a fruit sweeter than honey, they would most probably believe it on his testimony. But if one of the congregation had been there and tasted it, he would have a still stronger ground for believing it. In this state of things, suppose another was to come forward, and stoutly to deny that there was any such fruit. Those who believed it on the word of their minister might begin to doubt, in a greater or less degree, according to the trust they placed in him. But what would be the case with those who had actually *tasted* of the fruit? They would say, "Oh, you may talk, and it may seem very reasonable; but, though I cannot argue the matter with you, I *know* that you are wrong." So it is with those who have "*tasted* and *seen* that the Lord is gracious."

Such a temptation may assail you, even if you are one of God's children. And this may arise either from the weakness of your faith, which at best is but very small, and may for a season break down, or from conversing with some Infidel; or from reading some bad book; or you may be ill in body, and Satan may take advantage of this to molest your mind with blasphemous temptations. He is sometimes desperate, and uses desperate means to draw us aside. Now, in such a case, if you abhor the suggestion, it is well; and as long as you *do* abhor it, it will not condemn you. Instantly betake yourself to prayer. Wrestle with God. Humble yourself before Him. Entreat Him to root out the "evil heart of unbelief," and to give you that faith which can come only from Him. Treat it *as a temptation,* and meet it in God's strength. See that you are building on a sound foundation, and that you are resting firmly upon it. And then, if there be any shaking, though *you yourself* may be moved for a moment, your foundation will remain sure. It will only be as the reeling of the vessel safe at anchor, and not as the perilous dashing against the ruinous rocks.

But with regard to the resistance of temptation generally, remember that this is not done in an hour or a day. It is the work of *a whole life*—one continued warfare against sin. The power of temptation is felt more or less by every child of God, who "is passed from death unto life." And never will you be entirely beyond the reach of it, as long as you remain here.

But have you not many a *Promise* to encourage you? You are commanded, as I have shown you, to "resist the devil;" and with the Command comes the gracious Promise, "And he will flee from you." The moment you feel yourself tempted, or likely to be so, look up to a prayer-hearing God, and He will come to your help. Hide yourself under the shelter of His wings. "When the enemy shall come in like a flood, the Spirit of the Lord shall lift up a standard against him." (Is. lix. 19.) Your poor weak flesh may be ready to give way; but call to mind the words of Jesus to his tempted disciple—"Satan hath desired to have you, that he may sift you as wheat; but *I have prayed for thee* that thy faith fail not." Luke xxii. 31, 32.

This promise however will not hold good, if you *put yourself in the way of temptation.* For are you strong enough to stand against it? You may think so: but you are as little proof against it, as tinder is proof against the sparks which fall into it. Oh, if you love your soul, be very careful to keep out of harm's way. Do you not daily pray, "Lead us not into temptation?" Then beware how you wilfully expose yourself to it. If you really desire to shun the road of temptation, you are comparatively safe; but if you rush into it, and expect to escape unhurt, you are fatally deceiving yourself. You will be like the man in the gospel, "who fell among thieves; and they stripped and wounded him, and left him half dead." Solomon asks, "Can a man take fire in his bosom, and his clothes not be burned?" And, be assured, you cannot tamper with temptation, and come away unharmed.

Perhaps you are at times distressed to think that you should be so much tempted. The thought has more than once come across you, "Can I be a child of God, since Satan tries me so much?" Many a tempted believer has been greatly exercised with this thought. But let me tell you a few things for your comfort.

The *first* is, that God's children are *the very persons* whom Satan specially attacks. And perhaps it is because *you* are a child of God, that he so tries *you*.

The *second* is, that there is a great difference between *being tempted*, and *yielding to temptation*. Our Lord nowhere says, "Be not tempted;" but He does say, "*Enter not into temptation.*" The one is our *sin;* the other our *trial.* It is a sin to *welcome* the Tempter; but it is no sin to be *tried* by him. The Apostle does not say, "Blessed is the man who is *free from temptation,*" for such a man breathes not; but he does say, "Blessed is the man that *endureth temptation."* Joseph was tempted, and the holy Saviour himself was tempted; but neither of them yielded.

A *third* consolation for those who are tried by temptations is, that *Satan cannot tempt without God's permission.* Not one arrow can he shoot, not one drop of poison can he administer, unless God for some wise reason allows it. How is it in the works of nature? We sometimes watch the waves of the sea, roaring and dashing against the beach, and seeming as though they would threaten an inroad upon the shore. But their fury is under control; for "the Lord hath set a bound, that they may not pass over." Thus far they may go, and no farther. So hath he set bounds to Satan's power. "God is faithful," who will not suffer you to be tempted above that ye are able." 1 Cor. x. 13.

The *fourth* ground of comfort I will offer you is this—if temptation is permitted in your case, it is that it may serve as *a discipline for your soul.* In the School of Temptation we often learn much. It humbles us, makes us feel our weakness, and sends us to the Strong One for a better strength than our own. Temptation is to faith, what fire is to gold. The furnace not only discovers the true gold from the false; but it also makes the true gold purer. It becomes perhaps less in bulk, because everything worthless has been severed from it, but more in value. May *your* faith grow brighter and stronger by the trial! And being "much more precious than gold that perisheth, though it be tried with fire," may it be "found unto praise, and honour, and glory, at the appearing of Jesus Christ!" 1 Pet. i. 7.

Then, be cheered and encouraged. You have a Saviour; and He knows well what temptation is; and He can, and does, feel for his tempted people. "We have not an High Priest, which cannot be touched with the feeling of our infirmities, but was in all points tempted like as we are, yet without sin." (Heb. iv. 15.) Satan may lay his snares for you; but there is an almighty One near, who is watching over you, and who can shield you from all evil. The struggle may be severe and long. But if you have earnestly sought God's help, He will assuredly be with you, and will fight for you. Thus the victory will be yours; for it is written, "The God of peace shall bruise Satan under your feet shortly." Rom. xvi. 20.

CHAPTER XI.

DIFFICULTIES.

WEAKNESS OF FAITH.—A SENSE OF SINFULNESS.—WANDERINGS IN PRAYER.—THE DUTY OF CONFESSING CHRIST.—PERPLEXING PASSAGES OF SCRIPTURE.

THE very title of this book is encouraging—*The Pathway of Safety*. But you will perhaps think that I have said so much of the Christian's Dangers and Temptations, that I might well stop here, and turn to something a little more cheering.

But no; such was not our Lord's method. He concealed not one single difficulty from his beloved followers. He told them all they would have to encounter in their Christian course. And with this He mingled a joyful assurance, that He himself was with them, to strengthen them with his grace, and to carry them safely to their journey's end. And should

I be a faithful guide to you, if I only spoke to you of the happy home before you, and the pleasant objects by the way; and said nothing of the rugged path you are now and then called to tread, and the toils and trials you may chance to meet with by the way? Should I be a faithful guide, if I made *the pathway of safety* a downhill road, and the journey all sunshine? Why, your own experience, short as it is perhaps, will answer that question. It is far better that I should speak openly to you of your difficulties, and shew you the best way of meeting them.

You have difficulties of various kinds, I doubt not, even now, and many more you are sure to meet with. But before we go into particulars, let me say a word for your comfort. Others have met with them before you. God's dearest children have met with them in abundance. Nay, more, it is *good for us* to meet with them. The softest road is not always the best road. It is on the smooth ice we slip: a rougher path is usually safer for our feet. Our difficulties make us watchful. They plainly shew us our weakness, and send us to Christ for help. They humble us before God.

Now, let me mention a few of these Difficulties, which are likely to perplex you.

1. *Weakness of Faith.* This is what God's people oftentimes complain of. Perhaps when you first drew near as a penitent to Christ, you felt that He was all you needed, and your whole heart went out towards Him. There was an earnestness about you, which lifted you as it were above the world, and led you to accept with thankful eagerness the salvation offered to you. But now that the first fervour is over, you find so much weakness in your faith, that you are at times almost ready to doubt whether it is faith at all. "Oh, that I could get rid of this unbelieving heart," is your constant complaint.

My dear friend, it is well that you have begun to find out that in you "dwelleth *no good thing.*" The Christian's love—what is it at best? a poor and changing thing—sometimes warm and glowing, and at other times cold and weak! His obedience—how scanty! His faith —how weak and doubting! It was so with St. Peter. At one moment his faith was so strong, that he prayed, "Lord, bid me come unto thee on the water." And a few minutes after he was so weak that a little wind terrified him, and he cried out, "Lord, save me." We find him one day exclaiming, "Lord, I am ready to go with thee both into prison and to death;" and yet that very night he played the coward's part, and denied his Lord.

Learn then that everything on *your part* is, and must be, worthless and defective: all on *your Lord's part* is full and perfect. Learn also that it is not our Faith, but Christ, that saves us. Yes, He will save you, weak and helpless though you are, if you cast yourself unreservedly on Him.

But this littleness of faith distresses you. And yet that was no grief to you *once*. You had no misgivings *then* about your trust in Christ, because you had no trust at all. You once thought it easy to believe; for the only belief you knew of was a cold assent to the truths of the gospel, and a bare acknowledgment that Christ was your Saviour, but nothing more. This was easy enough; there was no heartwork in this. But now you feel faith to be a very difficult thing. The fact is, that when a man first endeavours really to believe at all, he discovers that this is beyond his power. And then he finds out to his sore grief the hardness and unbelief of his heart.

He earnestly desires to draw nearer to Christ, and to trust Him; but he discovers that what he formerly took for faith is utterly worthless —it deserves not the name of faith.

Then, surely, the very questioning in your heart is a sign of spiritual life, and that the Holy Spirit is indeed at work within you. It has been said, that "no man ever truly believed who had never doubted."

Consider from whence your faith comes. Not one single spark of real saving faith can be kindled in your heart but by God himself. Go then to Him day by day, and ask Him to give you the supply you so much need. Say, "Lord, I believe, help thou mine unbelief." "Lord, increase my faith." Be constantly looking to Christ, and lifting your heart above this world of sight. Oh, how difficult this is. But make the effort, and God will bless it. The very *attempt* to believe will be good for you. As a weak limb grows stronger by exercise, so will your faith be strengthened by the very effort you make in stretching it out towards things unseen. How was it with him who had the withered hand? When Jesus said to him, "Stretch forth thine hand," did he reply, "I have no power to do so?"

No, he made a great effort to thrust it forth; and in the very act of so doing, Jesus gave the needed strength. (Matt. xii. 10—13.) And now I say to you, Go and do *thou* likewise. Stretch out the poor weak hand of faith; and the more you do so the stronger will it become.

2. *A feeling of your great sinfulness* may also at times disturb you. You may say to yourself, "I am *too great a sinner* to be saved." But, as I observed in a former chapter, the time was when Satan tempted you with a very different bait. He then persuaded you that you had *no need* of a Saviour; that all was well with you; that your soul was in health; and so your sins gave you not the slightest concern. But now he is forced to change his ground with you. He will make you now feel, if he can, that you are *so desperately sinful*, that mercy cannot reach you. "Ah!" you will perhaps say, "if my sins were not so grievous, Christ would save me." But what says the word of God? "Though your sins be as scarlet, they shall be as white as snow; though they be red like crimson, they shall be as wool." (Isaiah i. 18.) You may well feel that your sins are great. But do not let this keep you from the Saviour.

No, my dear reader, this must not be; it should rather send you to Him.

Or, perhaps, your feeling is that, if Jesus was upon earth, you would then have some hope. You would go to Him, and cast yourself down at His feet, and entreat Him to save you. Listen, again, to God's word—that word which is the sinner's only guide—and what does it say? "Believe in the Lord Jesus Christ, and thou shalt be saved." Your Saviour is in heaven. There He sits at God's right hand. But He is just as able to save, and as ready to save, now, as He was when walking through the streets of Jerusalem. Believe in this unseen Saviour. Flee to Him in faith, and you will find Him waiting to receive you into the arms of His mercy. Saul of Tarsus believed on Him; the jailor at Philippi believed; hundreds have believed, and do believe, on Him; and their souls are saved. You may feel that your sins are great and numberless; but, great as they are, the power of Christ is greater. He is "able to save them *to the uttermost* that come unto God by Him." (Heb. vii. 25.) Paul was "the chief of sinners;" but he "obtained mercy"—and so will *you*, if you are making an earnest application for it.

There is also another mistake of the same kind which you may fall into. You may fancy that you must *make yourself acceptable* to Christ, by some act of goodness on your part, or by some course of preparation; that you must, in fact, *do something*, in order to make yourself *worthy* of Christ's salvation. What is this, but trying to set up a ladder of your own by which to climb heavenwards? Satan will look on, and rejoice. He will delight in seeing you toiling up it. But you will only be disappointed; for your ladder will most surely break from under you. No, you must come to the cross, stripped of all goodness, simply asking the Saviour to accept you *just as you are.*

Again, you may be tempted to think that by *waiting a little while*, you may perhaps be in a better condition for acceptance. Here is the same mistake, only under another form. And if Satan can but keep you from Christ, this is all he desires. The truth is, that, as long as we remain away from Christ, our condition only becomes worse and worse. If we were to wait for years, we could never *make ourselves worthy*. The only worthiness which He looks for, when He receives a penitent sinner, is a deep and contrite feeling of his own unworthiness. Would it, think you, be wise of the sick man, who is hastening to the grave, to say, when it is proposed to send for the physician, "No; wait a day or two, till I am better?" Would it be wise, if you had ruined yourself by your extravagance, and your creditors were making pressing demands upon you, and some one offered to pay all your debts, to say, "I will accept your kind offer when I am a little better off in the world. I am now too poor to accept it?" Is not the desperate nature of our spiritual sickness the very plea which we should urge for our Physician's help? Is not our destitution the very reason why we should apply for His immediate aid? And who so fit an object for the Saviour's mercy as a poor ruined sinner? Who so likely to be accepted of Him as one who feels undone without Him? The Publican did not wait. The Prodigal did not stay away till he felt worthy. He went with this very acknowledgment on his lips, "I am *not worthy* to be called thy son."

Christ is willing to save you, not for any goodness or fitness in yourself, but of His own free grace and mercy. He is willing to save you just as you are—sinful, worthless, undeserving. And it is those who feel this to be their state, who are welcome to the Saviour. "They that be whole," He says, "need not a physician, but *they that are sick*. I am not come to call the righteous, but *sinners* to repentance." Matt. ix. 12, 13.

Go, then, with the full burden of your sins, heavy though it be, and throw yourself at the feet of Christ. He loves to pardon the guilty, and to save the lost. No sin can be too great, no stain too deep, but that His blood can wash it out. (1 John i. 7.) Is He not the friend of sinners, and the Saviour of the lost? Then He is the very Saviour for *you*. Ask not that you may feel your sins less, but that you may feel His pardoning love more. Ask to be relieved, not only from the painful conviction of unforgiven sin, but also from its hateful power over you.

> From Calvary's cross a fountain flows,
>   Of water and of blood,
> More healing than Bethesda's pool,
>   Or famed Siloam's flood.
>
> The dying thief rejoiced to see
>   This fountain in his day:
> And there would I, though vile as he,
>   Wash all my sins away.

3. *Wandering in Prayer.* Here is another difficulty which is peculiarly distressing to God's children. You are not the only one who has had to mourn over it. Every one who prays feels it at times.

We kneel down in God's house, or in our own private chambers. We wish to speak to our Father who is in secret. And perhaps for a moment or two we really pray in earnest. Then, almost without our being aware of it, our attention flags. Some thought of quite another kind springs up, uncalled for, in our minds. And thus we presently find ourselves speaking to God with our lips, whilst our hearts are far from Him.

And it is very humbling to confess that sometimes *the most trifling* thoughts steal into our minds at such solemn moments. It is not that we are merely drowsy; that would be bad enough. But our thoughts fly off at times to matters of the most trivial nature. The world and sin still hover about us, even when we are upon our knees before God.

Now, is there any remedy for this? I believe there is; and if we use it, the evil will grow less and less, and we shall in the end master it.

First, look upon such wandering in prayer as *a direct offence* against God. Ask Him to forgive it for Christ's sake, and to grant you power to resist it.

Next, *watch against it beforehand.* Our Lord couples watchfulness and prayer together. He says, "Watch and pray." (Mark xiii. 33.) And St. Peter says, "Watch unto prayer." (1 Pet. iv. 7.) Try and get your mind into a serious frame *before you begin to pray.* For if you rush at once from your worldly occupations into God's presence, you will be pretty sure to have your heart full of them all the while: thus your mind will be distracted; and though your lips may pray, your thoughts will be roving elsewhere.

Set a watch too upon your heart *whilst you are praying.* Keep before you, all the while, the fact that you are speaking to a God who hears you, and that you are in His presence. Make prayer a *real* thing. You are confessing real sins. You are begging for real blessings. You really want to be heard and answered.

In this manner you may, with God's help, in some measure at least, remedy the evil. I do not say you will entirely overcome it; for I believe that few Christians, if any, have gained such perfect control over their thoughts, that at all times, when on their knees, they are able completely to shut out everything else, and to realise the presence of God only. But you may, by watchfulness and perseverance, do much towards keeping your mind clear of those worldly intruders, which so much disturb our devotions.

I ought perhaps to mention that the power of keeping the heart and mind fixed in prayer often depends upon the state of the body. Hence, in the time of sickness, or of any bodily suffering, how difficult it is to give the whole mind to prayer, or to any other spiritual exercise! Many have found this, and it has greatly distressed them. But let not such be discouraged. There is One above who can feel for us, and bear with our infirmities. Happy is it for us that He "knoweth our frame, and remembereth that we are dust."

4. I shall now call your attention to another point, on which many, who have just entered upon the hearty service of Christ, find a **difficulty**. " Ought I (they ask) to *declare openly the change in my feelings ?*"

You are perhaps living in a worldly family.

Those whom you are thrown among are, for the most part, worldly people. And such were you yourself lately: but now you are a candidate for heaven, and you are wishing to serve your new Master. "Ought I then (you will ask), to avoid observation, by keeping my feelings secret; or should I openly declare the change that has taken place in me?"

Perhaps the safest line to take will be this —Let men first see, by your *altered conduct*, that you are an *altered person*. And, then, if at any time you are spoken against for choosing the Lord's service, be ready to make a full avowal of what you feel. Bear the cross willingly, cheerfully, and fearlessly. But let the confession of a *holy life*, if possible, *come first*, for that is something real; and let the confession of the lips *follow*. It was well said by a Christian of former days, named Ignatius, that it is better for a man to hold his peace and *be*, than to say he is a Christian, and *not to be*." It becomes one in your condition to *say* but little concerning yourself. "Let your religion (as a Christian writer observes) be impressive by its consistency, and attractive by its amiableness. A word fitly spoken is valuable; but, in general, it is better for persons to *see* your religion than to *hear* it: it is better to hold forth the truth in your *life* than in your *language;* and by your *temper* rather than by your *tongue.*"

There are times however, when we *ought* to speak. And if, on such occasions, you shrink from the cross, and are ashamed of Christ and His service, this is a positive sin against your Lord. " The fear of man (we are told) bringeth a snare." (Prov. xxix. 25.) And so sure as we are cowards in our Master's service, and yield to the fear of reproach, we shall be kept from doing many things, which become us as His followers. It is not only your *duty* to confess Him manfully and openly, but it will be your *happiness* too. It will often be found a great relief to a young convert to unfurl his banner, and to let his character, as one who seeks heaven, be no longer concealed. This may cost you a struggle or two. But, when it is once done—when the bold step is once taken—many after-difficulties disappear.

I will give you an instance of this. A young naval Officer of my acquaintance became a truly religious man. At first he was naturally a little shy in his intercourse with his brother-officers. For a time he concealed his religious feelings, from fear of ridicule. Frequently, however, his conscience told him that this was wrong, and that he ought to declare the change in his views. So there was a daily struggle, a constant compromise between right and wrong; one moment a step forward, and then a step back, to save appearances, as though he had gone too far.

Happily a circumstance occurred which delivered him from this difficulty. It was the custom on board his ship, as it is in most, to have service every Sunday on deck. Now, it had long distressed him, that during the prayers no one knelt. He felt it was wrong, and the sin lay like a weight upon his mind. He determined, on the following Sunday, to do what he believed to be right, though in doing it he should act alone. So, when the general Confession was read, down he knelt. Instantly a look of astonishment, as he afterwards told me, proceeded from every eye. He was now a marked man. He had lost his character with the worldly. He was henceforth looked upon as a "methodist" and a "saint." He, no doubt, had to take up his cross, and bear something; but his course was now tenfold easier than it was before. He had come out in his true character, as a servant of God; and many of his former difficulties vanished away.

Whilst however it is your duty to make a manly avowal of "the good part" which you have chosen, I would again caution you not to be too free in *speaking of a change within*, lest your outward conduct should not bear sufficient evidence of it—not to be too forward in proclaiming yourself a servant of Christ, unless you have counted the cost, and have heartily entered upon His service. But when you have done this, when you have earnestly and decidedly chosen Christ for your Master, let there be no compromise, no desire to keep well with the world, no shrinking from the Saviour's cross; but a clear, bold, and upright walk in the heavenward path. " Whosoever," says our Lord, " shall be ashamed of me, and of my words, in this adulterous and sinful generation, of him shall the Son of man be ashamed, when he cometh in the glory of his Father with the holy angels." Mark viii. 38.

I am quite aware that there are many other difficulties which my Christian brother or sister will probably meet with in the journey to heaven. But I shall only mention one more.

5. In reading Scripture, you will find many *Difficult Passages* which you cannot understand. I have already (in the tenth chapter) called your attention to certain *disputed and doubtful questions*, which Satan often tries to busy us with; and these I have recommended you altogether to avoid. But I wish now to speak of those *passages of Scripture* which are "hard to be understood," and those *difficult doctrines* connected with God's truth, which must occasionally come before you.

These may perplex you. They are like steep places in your journey, and you may find a little difficulty in getting over them. You will perhaps wish to untie every knot, and to have all made plain to you. But why should you expect this? Does not God speak to us there of many deep things? And are we not very ignorant, even the wisest of us? How natural then that there should be much in the Bible beyond our reach!

When you come to a difficult chapter, or a **hard** verse, and, after a careful examination of it, you cannot understand its meaning, leave it for a while. You may, perhaps, as you read on, meet with some other passage which will throw light upon it. The more you read God's word, the plainer it will become to you.

Further, I would recommend you to dwell *chiefly* on those parts of the Bible which are the least difficult. Let these be your favourite study. Try to get a simple, child-like view of truth, and do not puzzle yourself with the more difficult matters.

It has been well said, that the best way to understand the difficult and mysterious doctrines in the opening of St. Paul's Epistles, is to begin to practise those plain rules and precepts which we find at the close of them. Set yourself to *practise* these; and then more *understanding* will be given you. The way to arrive at more knowledge is to obey what you already know. "A good understanding have all they that *do his commandments.*" Psalm cxi. 10.

A Lady of my acquaintance once fell into conversation with a Bricklayer. He told her that he was a good deal harassed about the doctrine of election. Her reply to him was a very sensible one. "When you build a house," she said, "do you begin with the chimneys? Do you not first concern yourself about the foundation? Well, now, you are a plain, simple man, and you are in earnest about your soul. Look well to the foundation then. Try and get a clear view of those great truths, which are plainly revealed to us. These are what you have chiefly to do with at present. Leave the high things of God for a while. They will all be made plain by degrees. The chimneys will come in their proper place." This was good and wise advice; and you, my reader, will do well to follow it.

There are many doctrines of the Gospel far beyond our reach. They are too high for our puny stature. They are not *contrary* to our reason, but they are *above* our reason. The doctrine of the Holy Trinity for instance, of the union of the Godhead and the manhood in the person of Christ, &c., are matters which we can neither hope to understand, nor attempt to explain. What then? Should we reject them, merely because they are beyond our comprehension? Or should we be disposed to murmur, because we are not as wise as God? Surely not: this would be folly. Let us be content simply to receive them, as truths which

God has made known to us. Let us accept them in humble faith; and not attempt to bring them down to the level of our own shallow understanding.

Meanwhile, wait humbly upon God. Read patiently and prayerfully His word. And the promise is, that " we shall know, if we follow on to know the Lord." (Hosea vi. 3.) " The meek will he guide in judgment, and the meek will he teach his way." (Psalm xxv. 9.) " If thou criest after knowledge, and liftest up thy voice for understanding; if thou seekest her as silver, and searchest for her as for hid treasures; *then shalt thou understand* the fear of the Lord, and find the knowledge of God; for the Lord giveth wisdom." Prov. ii. 3, 4.

Let it never trouble or surprise you that you sometimes meet with difficulties in Scripture. Rather be thankful that there is so much that is plain and easy. There are many dark things, that you will never comprehend fully here. But the dawn will soon break, and the shadows flee away. All will one day be light. " *Now,*" says the apostle, " we see through a glass darkly; but *then* face to face. *Now* I know in part; but *then* shall I know even as also I am known." 1 Cor. xiii. 12.

CHAPTER XII.

CAUTIONS.

**TRUE AND FALSE REPENTANCE.—AN UNSTABLE COURSE.
—RELIGIOUS EXCITEMENT.—FALSE TEACHING.**

To walk *boldly* along the path of life, is the Christian's duty and the Christian's happiness. But he must also "walk *circumspectly*." As a religious guide, I must not only urge you forward, but I am bound to caution you that you step carefully, lest you fall by the way. I shall therefore hold up a beacon or two, which I trust may be useful to the heaven-bound traveller.

The first caution I shall offer you, will be on the subject of *Repentance*. Now "Repentance" is a word very common in our mouths, but very often misunderstood. As the world takes it, it is a thing easily accomplished, and soon over. To be sorry for having done wrong—to leave off some of our most pressing sins—to attend to some duty that has been neglected—to resolve upon leading a better life—this is the beginning and ending of the repentance of many.

But, my dear reader, if God is working in your soul, I am very sure that your repentance will be something deeper than this. Think of past sin—the follies of your early youth, and those of your riper years—lost days, that cannot be gathered up—idle words, that cannot be recalled—wasted opportunities—broken vows and resolutions—sabbaths unimproved! Think what grace you have rejected in days past; how often you have resisted convictions; how carelessly you have felt towards Him who has so loved you; what a mere earthly life you have led; and how little you have thought of that better world before you! Think too how much has been wrong in you, *even since you fairly set your face Zionward;* how slowly you have opened your heart to Christ; how coldly and feebly you *have* served Him, and *are* serving Him now! Oh, are there not ten thousand thoughts that make your very heart bleed—ten thousand reasons why you should be humbled in the dust? You are still a sinner before God, and undeserving in His sight. And though the blood of Jesus Christ can wash out every stain; though there is a full and free, yea a *present*, pardon for you; and though you may have a humble assurance that you have obtained that pardon—yet you have need still to mourn deeply over past transgressions, and present shortcomings. Though there is forgiveness with God, there must be no forgiveness with *you*. I mean, you must not *forgive yourself*. It has been well said, that "repentance has a sort of double aspect; it looks upon things past with a *weeping* eye, and upon the future with a *watchful* eye."

Be not so anxious then to ask God to heal up your wound, as to probe it to the very bottom, even though it should give you much pain. Ask Him to grant you brokenness of heart, so that you may mourn over your sins with "godly sorrow." Awakened Christians are often so thankful for their deliverance, that they almost forget the pit from which the Lord in his mercy has brought them. They lose sight of their sin, in the joy of their forgiveness.

Do not mistake me. The Christian cannot

rejoice too much, when he beholds in Christ all he wants. He cannot feel His saving power to be too great. He cannot be too happy in the consciousness of being forgiven and accepted. You need not fear to trust too entirely to your Saviour. He has indeed paid the whole of your debt—all of it—to the uttermost farthing. He has borne the full weight of your sins in His own body on the tree. He has placed Himself completely in your stead, and has shed His life-blood for you. You do but honour Him then by accepting His salvation—by believing that every sin is washed away, and that you are eternally saved for His sake. But remember, oh remember daily and hourly, how undeserving you are. You have still much indwelling sin within you. You still need the constant cleansing of the Saviour's blood. This thought should deeply humble you.

Nothing passes with God for true repentance, but a thorough change of heart and life; ceasing to do evil, and learning to do well. When we discover our sin, it is not enough to confess it, and to mourn over it. We must forsake it utterly, and put it clean away. We must not only stop it in our actions, but pursue it home to our inclinations and desires, and dislodge it there: otherwise it will be all to little purpose; for the root being still left behind, it will surely shoot out again. Pray that you may, by the power of the Holy Spirit, gradually conquer this and that sin, and be ever aiming to be " holy as God is holy."

It is very important to bear in mind that this Repentance must be a *daily* work; for you have *daily* sins to be repented of. Your disease is for ever breaking out anew. And you have need to go again and again to the cross to seek forgiveness. Your life must be a *life of repentance*, and a constant looking to Christ for fresh grants of pardoning mercy.

Some may possibly call this a spirit of *bondage*. But truly that is a blessed bondage, which looses us from the chain of sin, and binds us closely to our Lord. You may be daily conscious of your sinfulness, and mourn over it before God; and yet you may have the fullest assurance of acceptance. You may be broken-hearted by reason of your unworthiness; and yet you may enjoy a peace that passeth all understanding, from the happy knowledge that Christ has put away your sin. A child does not cease to be a child, and become a slave, because he feels a keen regret for every act of disobedience to his loving father.

Think often of your sins, to humble you, and to keep you low. But also think often with thankfulness of that " Fountain open for sin and for uncleanness," where every stain can be washed away. (Zech. xiii. 1.) Then will you know the meaning of those words, " Sorrowful, yet alway rejoicing;" "Blessed are they that mourn, for they shall be comforted." 2 Cor. vi. 10; Matt. v. 4.

Next, let me warn you against an *Infirm and Unstable Course*. Stedfastness in religion is most important. Without it, we shall not do God's will heartily, or be really happy in His service. St. Paul felt this, when he said to the Corinthians, " Be ye stedfast, unmoveable, always abounding in the work of the Lord." (1 Cor. xv. 58.) On the other hand, the reproach of Reuben was, " Unstable as water, thou shalt not excel." (Gen. xlix. 4.) And St. James compares the unstedfast, or unstable, to the sea that is tossed about by every wind that blows upon it. "He that wavereth is like a wave of the sea, driven with the wind and tossed." James i. 6.

There are some who *begin* well. They make a good start, and promise fair. The green leaves come out upon the tree, the blossom bursts forth, but no fruit comes to perfection. Many persons go on in this state for years. They seem to be well disposed, and we hope that they will one day shew more firmness and decision. We look for fruit; but again and again we are disappointed. Thus they pass through the world, and perhaps leave it, in the same unsatisfactory state. And since our Lord has said, "He that is not with me is against me," we tremble for their souls.

Some again there are who seem to have accepted the promises of the gospel somewhat too easily. The truth was placed before them by their parents or teachers; and they received it *almost as a matter of course*, without any opposition or any doubting. They saw it was from God, and they embraced it. But there was never any great earnestness about them —never any very deep work in their souls. And what is the consequence? All is shallow and superficial. You talk to them of sin, and they willingly acknowledge that they are sinful and worthless. You speak to them of salvation by Christ, and they agree with you that "there is none other name under heaven given among men whereby we must be saved." They fall in with all you say; for they sincerely believe it to be truth. They cast in their lot with God's people; and we should be sorry to say that they are not His people; but they seldom or never become "burning and shining lights." You find them, time after time, much in the same state; and you cannot but see that there is a lack of earnestness and a feebleness of life about them. They are like plants in one's garden, which have never firmly taken root, and therefore never thrive.

Let not either of these be your character, dear reader. There should be stability and decision about the Christian. He should have his footing firm, and not be easily "moved away from the hope of the gospel." He should be "grounded and settled in the faith." (Col. i. 23.) His character should be stable; so that one may depend upon him as a religious man. There should be a vigour too about him, shewing clearly that Christ is his hope, and Heaven his aim.

Of course, we can hardly expect this of one who has only lately been brought to the knowledge and service of Christ. But what I would wish to urge upon you is, to aim at being stedfast, settled, and decided in your course.

Now, I know of nothing that will conduce more to this than going constantly to the Bible, as the great source of all your spiritual instruction. Learn your religion from *God*, rather than from *men*. Lay your foundation on the solid truth contained in God's word, and not on mere hearsay. "Thus saith the Lord,"—let that be your warrant for every doctrine which you hold, and for every command which rules your conduct. Stand upon that ground, and you are safe. Let God's Book be your main guide. Get your knowledge of His truth from that fountain-head. Draw water from that deep well, and you will feel the preciousness of every drop. Those who get their religious knowledge only from *books*, and from *conversation* with others, are for ever doubtful and wavering. They get a smattering of religious truth. They take up certain doctrines, because those whom they chance to be with have adopted them. But as they have not learnt them in God's school, and from His Word, and by His teaching, these doctrines lie only on the surface, and their minds have never laid hold of them. But it is not so with the *Bible*-Christian. Every stone of his building has been hewn out of God's quarry; and, therefore, it is solid, and will last. It may have cost a little more labour; but the work stands. The faith of such a Christian is not easily shaken. I mention this, because I have observed that Christians in the present day are a little disposed to lean upon books and tracts, and thus to slight the word of God. They perhaps find the doctrines of the gospel clearly stated for them in some nicely written book. This saves them trouble; and so they prefer it to God's word. Ah! we may get a smattering of truth in this way; but this is not drawing water from the deep wells of salvation. Take the bucket yourself, and fill it at the clear spring. Dig deep into the Scriptures, and *there* you will find solid gold. By such means alone can you become a sound and settled Christian.

An unstable member of any Body is a hindrance to it rather than a help. We want to reckon on the faithfulness and steadiness of those who belong to us. If I engage a Labourer to work for me, I like to feel that he is a sure man. If I buy anything at a shop, I like to go where I can depend upon the Tradesman. If a regiment of Soldiers goes out to fight for us, we like to feel that we can reckon upon their patriotism and their bravery. Seek, then, dear Reader, to be such a *Christian*, that men may be able to count upon your not flinching in the hour of trial, and not turning aside to the right hand or to the left.

Another thing I must caution you against is *Religious Excitement*. Not that you can be too much in earnest, or be too eager in pressing onward to heaven. Oh! no; the fire will not burn too warmly; the fear is lest it should become slack. Be earnest; but let there be a *staidness* and *sobriety* with your earnestness. Do not mistake mere warmth and excitement of the feelings for the work of the Spirit in the heart. The one will soon cool down, whilst the other will last.

I have witnessed some painful cases of this kind, where the feelings have been greatly moved, and the heart worked up for a time into a state of fever heat. And what is the consequence? Why, depression and coldness generally follow; the heart often sinks back into a state of greater deadness than ever; and the momentary peace it enjoyed is gone. For just as a fire, which is suddenly blown up into a flame, soon loses its brightness again, and becomes duller than before, and perhaps altogether dies out: so it will ever be with that soul in which mere excitement is allowed to take the place of quiet, genuine heart-earnestness.

It is much the same with the *body*. Stimulating spirits will give unusual strength for a moment; but they often leave the man weaker than before: whereas solid, wholesome food gives real and lasting strength to the frame.

Thus you see how Christians may deceive themselves. Be on your guard, then, lest you fall into this error. Do not run here and there, in the hope of winding yourself up to greater religious fervour. There is no real religion in this; it is worth nothing. It is only like counterfeit coin, which for a time may pass for true, but will soon be found out, and leave the owner poorer than ever.

But if you desire for yourself that warmth of feeling, strength of faith, and liveliness of hope, which will really last and steadily increase, depend upon it you will only obtain this by being much in prayer to God, by holding daily communion with Him, and by reading and meditating on His word. Thus He will lead you on from strength to strength, safely and surely.

Some people are easily excited and worked upon. And they especially have need to be on their guard. Let not too much dependence be placed on mere *inward feelings* of any kind. They are very treacherous and deceitful, very fitful and uncertain. A person may feel warmly under a stirring and affecting sermon, and go home determined to enter heartily upon the work of religion: heavenly desires may be kindled within him, and this world may seem, for the time, as nothing in his eyes. But if God has not touched the heart, that heart, like a tightly strung bow, will fly back the moment the string is loosed. All his bright and happy feelings will pass away; a wintry chill will come upon his soul; and it will end perhaps in his having reason to doubt whether he is a child of God at all.

Your religion then must not be *a mere religion of the feelings.* You must have something more solid to rest upon than the ever-varying pulse of your own frames and affections. See that there is a solid work of grace within you.

See that the fire is lighted by a flame from heaven. See that it is God's work, and not man's. Try to look out of yourself to Christ, and rest upon Him. Rely upon what *He has done for you*, rather than upon what you may *feel at the moment*. Let Christ be the object on which your eye is fixed. So will you be kept in " perfect peace," your " mind stayed upon Him." (Is. xxvi. 3.) For, whilst your feelings are like the weather-glass, constantly changing, He is like the sun in the heavens—He changeth not, but is "the same yesterday, and to-day, and for ever." Heb. xiii. 8.

Before I close the subject of Cautions, I feel that I should say a word or two about being led away by *False Teachers*. There are many of them in the world—Roman Catholics, for instance, and Mormonites, and Socinians, and numberless others. They may have a great deal to say. They may talk well, and thus mislead unstable souls. Beware of them. They will come to you with a show of truth. They will endeavour to unsettle your mind. They will very likely point out faults in your Church; or they will speak slightingly of your Minister, and try to shake your confidence in his teaching. They will perhaps open the Bible, and appear to base their arguments on Scripture; so did the great enemy when he tempted Jesus. They will seem to take a great interest in you; and they may really do so, for they may believe themselves to be right, whilst all the while they are in error. It was so with the Scribes and Pharisees of old: they "compassed sea and land to make one proselyte;" and no doubt theirs was an honest zeal, although they were "blind leaders of the blind."

Beware, then, of receiving too readily any new Teacher who presents himself. Beware of accepting any doctrine, merely because it is plausibly set before you, and because it *looks* like truth. " Beloved, believe not every spirit, but try the spirits whether they are of God; because many false prophets are gone out into the world." 1 John iv. 1.

The best safeguard in such cases is to be firmly established in the truth yourself. Let there be in you a solid scriptural foundation. Rest upon God's word. And trust fearlessly to those "old paths," and that "good way," by which your Church has guided thousands to a Home of Safety. If not, you will be easily pulled this way and that, and be tossed to and fro by every wind of doctrine. "Be fully persuaded in your own mind" as to the truths you hold. Let them be grafted there by the very hand of God; and then you need fear nothing from those who would mislead you, and move you off from your foundation. "Watch ye, stand fast in the faith, quit you like men, be strong." 1 Cor. xvi. 13.

CHAPTER XIII.

DUTIES.

TO GOD. — TO ONE'S FAMILY. — TO ONE'S FELLOW-CHRISTIANS.—TO THE WORLDLY.—TO THE HEATHEN.—TO ONESELF.

As a servant of Christ, you have not only dangers to avoid, and means of grace to help you on your way, and cautions to make you watchful, and promises to encourage you, but you have also DUTIES to discharge.

FIRST.—Our duty to *God* stands in the foreground. For one great difference between a worldly man and a Christian is this—the one considers that God has *a* claim, though not *the chief* claim upon him; the other feels that his duty to God stands out as the *one main object,* to which all else must give way.

And what is the duty which, as Christians, we owe to God?

1. We should *love Him* above all things. Even our nearest friends should not be dear to us, in comparison with Him. Thus David said, "Whom have I in heaven but thee? and there is none upon earth that I desire beside thee." Psalm lxxiii. 25.

Nothing short of God Himself will satisfy the soul, which has felt the emptiness of all earthly joys, and at last has found rest in Him. I say, nothing short of *God Himself.* The Christian's enjoyment of God may not be always the same. Sometimes it may be greater, and sometimes less. Sometimes his heart may be warmer towards God than at other times. But as the needle of the compass, when moved, ever turns to one particular point, and there fixes itself; so is God the one great object of attraction to the believer. There he finds a resting-place, and there alone does he love to dwell. The best of earthly things he cannot enjoy apart from God. He only enjoys them, as he enjoys God in them. Even spiritual gifts alone will not satisfy him; he wants *the Giver*, as well as *the gifts.* He desires Christ's presence as well as His ordinances. He knows that *the Fountain* is fuller than the stream, and *the Sun itself* more glorious than its rays.

This is a heavenly feeling indeed; and only grace can produce it within us. God Himself must plant this love in the barren soil of our hearts. He must "shed it abroad" there "by the Holy Ghost." Rom. v. 5.

How is it that we see some Christians working so hard for Christ, and serving Him so faithfully, and so happily? Their zeal never appears to flag; the fire within them never seems to cool. Let the watch you wear about you serve to answer the question. How is it that the hands are ever moving, and the little wheels always doing their work? What puts them all in motion? Look closely, and you will discover a strong, but almost unseen, spring that sets all agoing. Take away that mainspring, and the watch is useless. And there is something too within the Christian, which secretly moves his heart, his affections, and his desires. Love is the Christian's mainspring. "We love Him, because He first loved us;" "The love of Christ constraineth us."

Be constantly asking yourself, Do I love God with all my might? Is my love on the increase? Do I love Him supremely—above all other objects? Specially ask God to endue you with this holy principle of love. Pray that you may love Him, not *sometimes*, but *always;* not *a little,* but *with the whole heart.* Let your love be firm and constant—not coming and returning, like the tide; but flowing on, like a river, with a full and even course.

2. We should *live to God.* Our love if it is true love, will be sure to produce obedience, and devotedness, and submission to God's will. We should feel that our little short life may well be spent in His service, and to His glory. "Ye are not your own," says the inspired Apostle; "for ye are bought with a price: therefore glorify God in your body, and in your spirit, which are God's." (1 Cor. vi. 19, 20.) We are not sent into this world, as many seem to think, merely to eat and drink, and get our living, and pass our time as may be most pleasing to ourselves. We are sent here for a great work—to obtain salvation for our souls, to glorify our Lord, and to serve Him in our day and generation. Christ has laid down His life for us; and in return for so vast a benefit, we should give our lives to

Him. "He died for all, that they which live should not henceforth live unto themselves, but unto Him." 2 Cor. v. 15.

Most of us in these days are called, not to any one great act of heroism or self-sacrifice; but Christ calls us to a life of active daily duty, and in such a life we may best glorify Him. But, oh, how difficult to live such a life! To carry out the humble duties of each day, with cheerfulness and contentment—to keep up the warmth of our piety amidst the cold and deadening cares and occupations of the world—to do everything as for God, and to have a high and holy end before us, even in our lowliest toils—this, as has been well said, needs a faith as strong as that of the man who dies with the song of martyrdom on his lips. Truly it is a great thing to love Christ so dearly, as to be ready to *die* for Him; but it is often a thing not less great to be ready to take up our daily cross, and to *live* for Him.

If you are a true Christian then, you will *love God* and *live unto Him.* And remember this—you cannot live *to* God in the world, unless you live much *with* Him, apart from the world. You cannot feel real devotedness to His service, unless you are in the constant habit of drawing near to Him in meditation and prayer. This is the secret of a holy, happy life devoted to God's service.

SECONDLY.—Next to God comes *your own Family*. You have a most important and interesting duty to discharge to them. It is a happy thing for you, if the other members of your family are of the same mind as yourself, if they feel with you on religious subjects, and are seeking with you the way to heaven. *Then* there is a stronger cord that binds you together than even that of nature. And, in this case, your difficulties will be few, and your course comparatively smooth.

But I will suppose it otherwise. Perhaps you stand alone in your family: the rest are for the world, you are for God. Those, to whom you would naturally look for a helping hand, are rather disposed to check you. Those, whom you have hitherto regarded as your counsellors in everything, seem now to be a little alarmed at your earnestness, and would put a clog upon your wheels, instead of urging you onward.

Now, if this be the case, do not fly off from them, and take a solitary course of your own. But try to act in accordance with their wishes, as far as you are able to do so, without wounding your own conscience. Certainly, you must obey God rather than man, in things which He clearly commands. But never act in *needless* opposition, especially where a Parent is concerned. Show them that it is not for opposition's sake that you differ from them, and that it gives you real pain not to fall in with the opinion of those, whom, in other matters, it is your delight to obey and follow. Let them see by your dutiful and affectionate conduct towards them, and by your readiness to meet their wishes, that you love them just as much as before; yea, more warmly than ever, for Christ's sake.

So too with the other members of your family circle. It may be, they thwart and oppose you in your religious path. But cheerfully bear every taunt. Return with kindness every hard word. Remember what you once were yourself. Does not our Lord say, " I came not to send peace, but a sword"? And does He not even foretell that "a man's foes shall be they of his own household"? (Matt. x. 34, 36.) *You* may be now feeling the truth of this. Once all was harmony and agreement in your family; but now a difference of opinion on the most vital points has sprung up. Unkind remarks are constantly made about your religious views; and your actions and feelings are often mistaken. Well, so it always has been; so it was with Christ; and so it may be now with you. But does not the Lord bid His followers to take up the cross, and bear it after Him? *This* is one part of that cross; and will you not bear it gladly, patiently, meekly, for His sake?

Now, let it be your earnest endeavour to be a peace-maker in your family. Whenever anything goes wrong, throw in if possible a healing, soothing word. Many a little bickering may thus be stopped. And the quiet, gentle, Christian spirit which you are enabled to shew will be sure to have its influence on all about you. Try to win over every member of your family to the Lord's side. Try by gentle means to lead them into the same pleasant path, into which you, through God's mercy, have been brought. It is far better to attract them by the holiness and blamelessness of your conduct, and to draw them with the silken cord of love, than to try and force them by warmth of argument, and by condemning them for what perhaps they do not yet see to be wrong. Endeavour to *win* them to Christ by your words, but still more by your example. There are a thousand little acts of affection you may daily show them, and a thousand ways in which the beautiful fruits of religion may display themselves. Be cheerful and kind among them. Love your home, and try to make it happy to all.

Our religion, if it is true religion, will make us feel more warmly than ever towards our relatives. God never intended that it should snap asunder these earthly bonds, but rather strengthen them. He will never blame us for loving *them* too much, but for loving *Him* too little. Let it not be thought that in giving your heart to Christ, you are weakening your affection to your family, but rather deepening it.

I once knew a young man, a member of a large family. His duty called him into a foreign country, and whilst there it pleased God in His great mercy to touch his heart, and to awaken serious feelings within him. When his mind became religiously impressed, one of his first thoughts was, "What will they think of me, and say of me, at home?" He boldly wrote to his father, telling him that his mind and feelings were greatly changed. But still he wrote in the spirit of meekness, and as one who needed rather to be guided, than to guide and teach others. On his return home, the same humble and affectionate spirit marked his conduct, and the same dutiful deference to his parents. There was a cheerfulness, too, about his manner, which shewed that the religion which had rooted itself in his heart was not a religion of gloom, but one which produced peace within, and had a happy influence on others.

Here was a beginning of larger blessings to that family, a light set up to shine in it. And God blessed that young man's quiet, consistent example, and heard his prayers; so that he had the happiness of seeing first one, and then another, taking the same serious view of things that he had taken himself.

Now, if he had pursued another course; if he had been sharp and uncharitable towards those about him; if he had borne impatiently any little opposition he might occasionally have met with; if he had tried to *force* his views upon others, instead of gently *persuading* them; he might not only have lost much of the peace which he himself enjoyed, but those most dear to him might have been checked in their religious course, rather than led on, by his example.

If you should find yourself in the same situation as this young Christian, endeavour to act as he did. This is the surest and happiest course to take, and one that God will most certainly bless.

But this book may, perhaps, fall into the hands of some Christian *Parent*. Oh! what deeply interesting and affecting duties *you* have to discharge—to order your household in the fear of the Lord, and to bring up your children for Him. But it must be enough for me merely to hint at these most important duties. Remember, your position is a most responsible one. Every child is a precious talent committed to your care. See that you employ it, as one who must give an account. Endeavour to be a spiritual, as well as a natural, Parent to your children; aye, to take more care to get a portion for their souls in heaven, than to make provision for their bodies on earth.

What a difference there is in family circles; and how much of that difference may depend on the Parent! Think of that Family at Nazareth, of which Jesus was a member. What a happy home it must have been! And if we were only more like Him, how many happy homes would there be in our own land! " But there are, we fear (observes a Christian writer), many *un*happy homes—many wretched families —more by far than is generally supposed. And what is the cure for this? The presence of Jesus. Oh, let Him into your houses, to dwell with you, and form one of your family circle, and He will turn your homes into little Edens; He will heal your divisions; He will banish sadness and sorrow; He will cement you into one holy, happy family; and then will be realized all that imagination ever conceived of the charms of home. He would fain enter into our homes, if we would let him. Believe me, it is His presence that sanctifies and sweetens domestic life. Without this it is a poor thing. Many fine things have been said of domestic bliss; but rest assured that the presence and love of Jesus is the sweetest drop in the cup, and that without this it will speedily turn into gall and wormwood."

It has often been said, that Charity should begin *at home ;* and may we not also say that Piety should begin *at home ?* The man in public is not always the same man in private;

but the good man—the Christian man—in private will be sure to be the Christian man in public.

THIRDLY—Towards *your Fellow-Christians* also you have a special duty. "Love *the Brethren,*" is the Apostle's precept. And it was said of the early Christians, even by the heathen, "See how these Christians love one another." They are God's people; they belong to Christ; and if you love *Him,* you will love *them* also. This special love towards the children of God is a mark which always belongs to His family: "We know (says the beloved apostle) that we have passed from death unto life, because we love the brethren." 1 John iii. 14.

Learn to bear with the faults and failings of your fellow-Christians. They are not perfect, they have many infirmities—and remember how great, and how many, are your own. Never be jealous of them, if they are preferred before you, or are more noticed than yourself. When you hear a Christian brother or sister highly spoken of, it should give you real pleasure; and instead of thrusting in a word by way of lessening the praise bestowed upon them, you should rejoice that they are honoured. Again, never try to exalt yourself above others. It was the sin of Diotrephes, that "he loved to have the preeminence." How much more Christ-like is it to be willing to take the lower place, and to "esteem others better than yourself"—being "kindly affectioned one to another with brotherly love, in honour preferring one another." Shew your brethren much kindness for Christ's sake. Is it not written, "Whosoever shall give to drink unto one of these little ones a cup of cold water only in the name of a disciple, verily I say unto you, he shall in no wise lose his reward;" and again, "Let us do good unto all men, especially unto them who are of the household of faith." Matt. x. 42; Gal. vi. 10.

One too often sees a lack of kindness and love even among God's people. You mourn over it perhaps, and wish it otherwise. But do not stop there. Take *your* part at least in promoting a more tender loving spirit among your Christian brethren—remembering always His words, who said, "This is my commandment, that ye love one another as I have loved you."

FOURTHLY—But the Christian has a duty to perform towards *those whose hearts and hopes are in this present world.* And this is sometimes very difficult; so much so that St. Paul gives a special caution respecting it, " Walk in wisdom toward *them that are without.*" (Col. iv. 5.) To despise those who knew not Christ, is clearly wrong; for let us remember that there was a time when we ourselves knew Him not. To shun and avoid them is also wrong; for we may by God's blessing do them good. But to throw ourselves into their society, and to fall in with their ways, is to endanger our own souls.

There is a safe line which may be drawn, so as to keep clear of each of these errors. Seek as much as possible the companionship of the godly. Let *these* be your friends and associates. And when you chance to be thrown in with worldly persons, be careful to say nothing, and to do nothing, which may give needless offence. Without falling into Peter's sin, and shrinking from owning whose you are, try to win your way by cheerfully and good-naturedly bearing any reproachful words, which may be spoken against you; and at any rate shew a kind spirit towards those who differ from you. Make great allowances for others; try to do them good; and above all, earnestly pray for them. A gentle and forbearing manner often finds the way to a man's heart, which has been long barred and closed against the most powerful attacks; as the warm sunbeam, without any noise or violence, induced the Traveller in the fable to cast off his cloak, which all the blustering of the wind could not do, but rather made him gather it closer, and bind it faster about him.

With the fixed determination then, by God's help, to keep your own straight, consistent, Christian course, and to let nothing turn you from it, conduct yourself with all humility and love towards those, who are following the world instead of Christ, and use every effort in your power to lead them into a better path.

FIFTHLY—You have also a duty *to the Heathen.* Many turn away from them, and say with Cain, " Am I my brother's keeper ? " But it must be far otherwise with you. You feel the rich blessings of the gospel; and do you not long to bring many, yea all, within its sound? You know what it is to have a Saviour to flee to, and to love: then think of those to whom that Saviour is unknown. Give what you are able, though the sum be small, to some Missionary Society. And if you find it a difficult matter to spare even that small sum, deny yourself, so that you may, by that means, have something to give. Thus will you enjoy the happiness of contributing your little portion towards sending ministers of the gospel to those who know not Christ; and you yourself will be helping to "guide their feet into the way of peace." Endeavour also to stir up others to take a part in this blessed Christian work.

Sixthly—And now, is there not a further duty, which you owe to *Yourself?* You have a soul to ripen for heaven; and you have a Christian character to maintain whilst you are here.

A soul to ripen for heaven! What an important work! You are living in the midst of a deadening and ensnaring world. God has kindled a flame in your soul; and the fire must be kept up, or it will soon burn but very dimly; for the cold, damp atmosphere of the world is all against it. How can this be done? By continued watchfulness, and by applying daily and hourly to Him in whom all fulness dwells; by using all the means of grace; and by living a life of faith on the Son of God. "I know (said good Bishop Beveridge), I know that I must *strive*, before I can enter in at the strait gate. I must *win* the crown, before I can *wear* it. I must be a member of the Church *on earth*, before I can be admitted into the Church *in heaven*. In a word, I must go through a solitary wilderness, and conquer many enemies, before I come to the land of Canaan, or else must never be possessed of it."

A spirit of self-denial too is needed, if we would grow in conformity to our Lord, and ripen for His presence. But oh, how feebly do we often run our race! How little exertion do we make to win our prize! What a soft, easy life do many Christians of the present day live! Many of us seem to fancy, that, if we know the truths of the Gospel, and believe them, and embrace them, nothing more is needed—that our work is done. But can this be ripening for heaven? Can this be the religion of Christ? Must we not have mistaken the Gospel? For what says our Lord? "If any man will come after me, let him deny himself, and take up his cross daily, and follow me." Luke ix. 23.

Remember, then, the cross must be taken

up; not once or twice, but *daily*. We must not shrink from it, because it galls us, but be content cheerfully to bear it. We must daily exercise some act of self-denial. Instead of doing a thing, because it is pleasing to flesh and blood, we must ask ourselves, " Is it pleasing to *God?* " and if not, we must at once put a yoke upon our own will. Our desires, our intentions, our actions, must all be brought into captivity to the obedience of Christ.

In short, dear reader, there must be a daily course of self-denial, if you would reach heaven—a daily dying to self, that you may live to God—a daily renouncing your own pleasure, that you may please your Lord—thinking nothing too dear to give up, nor anything too hard to bear, for Him who counted not His life too dear, nor the cross itself too heavy to bear, for you.

And you must practise this self-denial in *little things*, as well as in *great things*. For it is in the every day acts of life that the true Christian should shew himself; and it is not so much on special occasions, but in the ordinary path of duty, that he most honours God by a cheerful, happy obedience to His will. Without this we cannot be growing, and ripening, and becoming fit for our Master's presence.

But further, you have *a Christian character to maintain* whilst you are here. Christ has called you to His service. You have enlisted under His banner. You are one of His people. Then, be sure the world's eye is upon you. It will closely watch your course. It will mark every false step. The Christian is spoken of as a "city set upon a hill;" as "a light" that may be seen; as an "epistle of Christ, known and read of all men." How anxious you should be then in no way to dishonour your Christian profession; but to display a holy and blameless character in the world which you are living in! How carefully you should avoid even the appearance of evil! You may do immense harm to the cause of Christ by one unguarded word, by one false step, by one unbecoming act.

Pray that God may keep you in the strait and narrow path—that He may uphold you by His own grace; for most assuredly you will fall, if He supports you not. Pray too that He may enable you to "let your light so shine before men, that they may see your good works, and glorify your Father which is in heaven." Matt. v. 16.

CHAPTER XIV.

ENCOURAGEMENTS.

This is a brighter and more welcome subject. And happily the anxious Christian need not look far for *Encouragements*. His journey may have been wearisome and difficult, but he has abundant comforts by the way. If he is in *the pathway of safety*, there is many a refreshing spring by the roadside to cheer him. He may "drink of the brook in the way," and thus be enabled to "lift up the head." Psalm cx. 7.

How many sweet and precious promises in God's Word are made *specially to him!* He may take them to himself, and derive abundant encouragement from them. The Bible is like "the pillar of the cloud," which followed the Israelites: it was all light to them; but it was all darkness to the Egyptians. (Exodus

xiv. 20.) So the Scriptures speak with a voice of cheering encouragement to God's children; but they are full of threatenings to the worldly. Be of good courage then, my fellow-Christian, and go on your way rejoicing. I am permitted to address you with words of encouragement.

1. *God is* YOUR *God.* You were brought into covenant with Him in baptism. And since that time you have deliberately chosen Him as your portion. What an unspeakable blessing to be permitted to say of Him who made the world, and rules in heaven—of Him who is all-wise and all-mighty—this God is *my* God!

Seek to realize God's presence as much as possible. Believe that He is near you, with you, by your side, though you see Him not. Wherever you are, and whatever you are doing, remember that God is there. Speak often to Him. Converse with Him as with a Friend. Hold communion with Him. Lift up your heart to Him constantly. This is "walking with God," as Enoch walked. Gen. v. 22.

And who can tell the blessedness of such a walk? You will enjoy a peace which the world cannot disturb. Its troubles and vexations may come close to you, but they cannot hurt you. You may take them as your appointed portion, without being distressed by them. You may even look down upon them, and smile at them, with the happy feeling that they will soon pass away, like clouds that will presently give place to a bright and lasting sunshine.

Look upon God as your *Father*. This is your privilege. This blessed feeling of relationship will draw out your confidence and affection towards Him. He is your *Father;* and therefore *He will deny you nothing* which is for your good. "He that spared not his own Son, but delivered him up for us all, how shall he not with him also freely give us all things?" (Rom. viii. 32.) He is your *Father;* and therefore *all that He does must be well.* This will reconcile you to every trial, and sweeten every pain. Again, He is your *Father ;* and will you not feel it *your greatest pleasure to do His will*—not in *some* things, but in *all* things—not in great things merely, but also in each little work of life?

Oh, cherish this idea, that God is indeed your *Father;* and this will make every duty pleasant, and every burden light. Daily and hourly call this relationship to mind. For instance, is the Bible spread out before you? Say to yourself, " It is *my Father's book;* it is His voice that speaks to me in it; here He makes known to me exactly what He would have me do." Are you going to church? Let this thought be in your mind, " It is *my Father's house.* There will He be to meet me; to hear all my wants; to listen to my voice, as I pour out my thanks; and to give me directions as to the course He would have me follow." Does affliction come to you? Comfort yourself with the feeling, " It is *my Father's rod:* I will kiss it as it smites me." Are you called to some difficult work, which you plainly see to be your duty? Say to yourself, " It is *my Father's business:* I will cheerfully engage in it for His dear sake." Are your plans crossed and thwarted? " *So my Father orders it:* His will be done ! "

> "It was thy will, my Father,
>   That laid thy servant low ;
> It was thy hand, my Father,
>   That dealt the chastening blow.
>
> " It was thy mercy bade me rest
>   My weary soul awhile ;
> And every blessing I receive
>   Reflects thy gracious smile."

2. *Jesus is* YOUR *Saviour.* He is not merely *a* Saviour, but He is *your* Saviour. If you heard of some one who was rich, and kind, and benevolent, you would doubtless have a feeling of great respect for him. But if that same person had been kind *to you*, would you not have a still warmer feeling towards him? And can you not *now* say of Christ what you could not *once* say—" My beloved is *mine,* and I am his. He loved *me,* and gave himself for me?" Cant. ii. 16; Gal. ii. 20.

Live upon Christ daily and hourly. Have an eye to His glory in everything. Let your life be a life of faith. Walk "as seeing Him who is invisible." (Heb. xi. 27.) You have fled to the Saviour for pardon and acceptance. You have found Him. Now live upon Him day by day. Pray that St. Paul's experience may be more and more yours:—"I live, yet not I, but Christ liveth in me; and the life which I now live in the flesh I live by the faith of the Son of God." Gal. ii. 20.

You are now united to Christ. You are, I trust, a living branch of the true Vine. (John xv. 5.) See that you are not drawing your nourishment from other sources, but from Him only. There are some plants which we see growing up against our walls, whose branches are nourished from the parent stem. But, in addition to that, they will, wherever they can, send out little roots of their own, and so draw nourishment for themselves in more ways than one. Now, we sometimes see this very thing taking place among professing Christians. They are not satisfied with the support they obtain from the true Vine; but they are for ever sending out little roots of their own to draw nourishment from other sources.

Carefully destroy all such roots, wherever you find them shooting forth, and see that all your support comes from Christ. Let there be a constant chain of prayer linking you on to Him, and drawing you nearer and nearer to Him. Let your "life be hid with Christ in God." (Col. iii. 3.) Rest on his promises. Feed on Him as your spiritual food. Draw constantly from His fulness, and ever be looking to Him as the deliverer and sustainer of your soul. Cling to Him, as closely as the limpet clings to the rock, both for safety and for sustenance.

After all, what is true religion? It is not so much a belief in certain doctrines, or a holding of certain opinions, as it is *a cleaving of the soul to a living, loving Saviour.* This is the religion that lasts. This is the religion that sustains the soul, and gives it peace and joy.

Blessed are you, if you are thus living on Christ. " Thus only (says a Christian minister) can we be sustained amidst all the trials of life. Are we weary? We can lean, like St. John, upon the Saviour's bosom. Are we burdened with a sense of sin? We can hide in the clefts of that Rock of ages. Are we empty? We can look to Him for an immediate supply. Are we hated of all men? We can shelter ourselves under His wings. Stand on the Lord Jesus as your foundation, and then you may smile at Satan's rage, and face a frowning world."

This is the secret of a really happy Christian course. Here is the spring of all growth and progress. Why do so many *begin* well, and nothing more? They get to a certain point, and there they stop. They have fled to Christ, perhaps, and have found peace in Him. But they do not *go on to live upon Him;* and therefore there is no advance. They sink down wearied, instead of running the Christian race.

Remember, then, Christ is *your* Saviour, and *your* Friend. He is on your side, for you have given yourself to Him. And, through Him, you will be sustained under every trial, and will overcome every difficulty.

3. *The Holy Spirit too is* YOUR *Guide and Comforter.* If you were journeying in a strange land, you would need a Guide to point out the road, to lead you into the right track, and to help you over the difficulties of the way. And is not this world *a strange land* to you? Thank God, there is a safe road through it—a beaten track. But no one ever found it of himself. The Holy Spirit is ready to be your *Guide.* He can take of the things of Christ, and "shew them to you." He is ever ready to "lead you into all truth." (John xvi. 13, 15.) You have the Bible; but that will be but a closed book, unless the Holy Spirit unfolds its meaning to you, and sheds His own light upon it. Look to Him then daily as your *Guide* and *Teacher.*

And further apply to the Holy Spirit as your *Comforter.* Your heart will often ache. Sorrow will often cross your path. Earthly comforts will soon dry up. They are but poor remedies, when the wound is within. But the Spirit of God can refresh your soul. He can lead you beside those "still waters," where you may find the truest peace.

4. *The Saints of God are* YOUR *fellow-travellers.* Here is a further encouragement. You are not a solitary pilgrim along the journey of life. There are many with you. A goodly band have already reached the happy country : " through faith and patience " they "inherit the promises." And others are struggling on; fighting against the same enemies, and meeting with the same dangers and difficulties as yourself. Take courage then. The strength that supports them in their weakness shall support you. The same " everlasting arms" are underneath you. The same shield, which protects them, shall be your defence. The same victory shall be yours.

But it may so happen, that there may be none of your own friends journeying on the same heavenly road as yourself. The Lord may have seen fit to cast your lot in a place, or fix you in a family, where you may not find any with whom you may take sweet religious counsel. Let not this however dishearten you, or lead you to exclaim, "Who will show me any good?" But rather make the Psalmist's prayer your own, "Lord, lift *Thou* up the light of thy countenance upon me." (Ps. iv. 6.) If you experience constant nearness to God through the Spirit, and are warmed by communion with Christ, it matters little whether you travel to heaven alone, or in company.

5. *The Home which some of God's children have reached is* YOUR *Home.* Sometimes we are ready to sink beneath our heavy burden. But why so? It is true, this is the scene of our labours. This is the land of trials and of sorrows. But our resting-place is near—our home—our Father's house. Jesus has purchased it for us. He is gone there himself to "prepare a place" for us. Our loving Father bestows it upon us as our inheritance. "Fear not, little flock; it is your Father's good pleasure to give you the kingdom."

Yes, we have abundant Encouragements. And yet, how is it there is so little *pressing* into the kingdom? Why are there so many *professors*, and so few *Christians*—so many that "*run*," and so few that "obtain"—so many who *go into the field* against Satan, and so few who come out *conquerors*—so many who *wish* to reach the happy land, but never *gain* it? It is because they do not trust God. They do not "wait upon the Lord," and thus "renew their strength." And what is the consequence? They have no power to grapple with the difficulties that meet them on their way to happiness. They leave heaven to others, who will venture all for it. Like Orpah, they go a little way with Christ, and then, when hardship stares them in the face, they leave Him; loath to lose heaven, but more loath to buy it at so dear a price.

But I hope better things of you, my dear reader. Is there not a voice which speaks to you from heaven—a voice from One who loves you and feels for you? And that voice is ever whispering to you and saying, "Be thou faithful unto death, and I will give thee a crown of life." There is a peaceful and happy life before you here, and a heaven hereafter. These are your portion—this is your inheritance. Oh, forfeit it not through lack of faithfulness.

It is true, there are many *Dangers* in your path; but I have shown you where you can find a shelter. There are *Difficulties* which you will meet with; but I have also told you of strength that will support you under them, and bring you through them. I have spoken of *Enemies,* too, whom you will have to encounter; but, you see, there is a matchless armour provided for you. And, thanks be to God, He can "give you the victory through our Lord Jesus Christ." 1 Cor. xv. 57.

> Strong in the Lord of hosts,
>   And in his mighty power,
> Who in the strength of Jesus trusts
>   Is more than conqueror.
>
> From strength to strength go on;
>   Wrestle, and fight, and pray;
> Tread all the powers of darkness down,
>   And win the well-fought day.
>
> Then, having all things done,
>   And every conflict past,
> Ye shall behold your victory won,
>   And gain the crown at last.

CHAPTER XV.

PROGRESS AND RELAPSE.

Did you ever, from day to day, watch the growth of a crop of corn? First, the seed is sown. After a while, the green shoots make their appearance above the surface. The blade, week after week, grows higher and stronger, though continually checked by frost and cutting winds. Then the ear is formed, and the grain swells within it. At length the crop loses its green colour, and a bright golden yellow takes its place. We now see that it is ripening. The warm rays of the sun are daily and hourly bringing it to perfection; till at length the sickle sweeps it down, and it is gathered into the barn.

Is this a picture of yourself, dear reader? Does this describe your gradual, steady growth—your spiritual ripening—your increasing meetness for the heavenly garner? Look at St. Paul: how was it with him? What earnest desire there was in him to be getting on, to be making progress, to be advancing towards heaven! He *ran*, he *fought*, he *trained himself*, he *strove* eagerly for the prize. Hear his own words; "I therefore so *run*, not as uncertainly; so *fight* I, not as one who beateth the air; but *I keep under my body*, and bring it into subjection." "Forgetting those things that are behind, and reaching forth unto those things that are before, *I press* toward the mark." Phil. iii. 13, 14; 1 Cor. ix. 26, 27.

And so it will be with every one in whose soul there is spiritual life. If, for instance, you feel sin to be a hateful thing, you will be ever taking a closer and deeper search after it; and you will be longing to clear out all that is evil in your heart. If, again, you have faith to believe in Christ, you will be seeking for *more* faith; you will be daily praying to have it *increased*. If you know something of God, you will be anxious for *further and fuller* knowledge of Him. If His love has been " shed abroad in your heart," you will not be content with what you have got; but you will feel that you want *more*. If, in short, you have taken some steps up the ladder, you will desire to be mounting *higher and higher*.

Now that you have welcomed Christ to your soul, let there be a daily and steady advance. You have gained much; but there is still more to win. You have touched, as it were, the hem of the Saviour's garment, and been healed by Him; but do not shrink back into the crowd again. "As ye have received Christ Jesus the Lord, so walk ye in him, rooted, and built up in him, and stablished in the faith." (Col. ii. 6, 7.) It is not enough to have drawn near to Christ: you must learn now to *live with Him*—not to be content with His presence just now and then, but to desire it always; to do everything as if He was by your side. "I must (said a good old Christian minister) acquire the holy habit of connecting everything with God. Whether my affairs move on smoothly or ruggedly, God must be acknowledged in them. If I go out of my house, or come in, I must go out and come in as under the eye of God. If I am occupied with business all the day long, I must have the glory of God in view. If I have an affair to transact with another, I must pray that God would be with us in that affair, lest we should blunder, or injure, and ruin each other."

Such a heavenly state as this is within our reach; and we should try to attain to it. But it may be asked, "Are those who are thus advancing always the first to see their own progress?" No; I believe not. Oftentimes the Christian grows, without knowing it himself. He may even fancy that his heart is getting worse instead of better; because he sees the greatness and the number of his sins more clearly, and feels them more keenly. He may think that his faith is weaker than ever; because he discovers more painfully his unbelief. In short, the more he grows in grace, the lower he sinks in his own eyes. Once he thought well of himself; but he has learnt to take a humbler view of his state before God: just as the blade of corn shoots up boldly, and the young ear raises its head with confidence; but, as it becomes fuller, it droops towards the ground, not because it is feebler, but because it is heavier and riper.

It often happens too that a Christian's growth may be slow, and yet real. Do we *see* the corn rise in the fields? Do we *see* the hour-hand of the clock move? Yet in each case there is sure and gradual progress. Oh that it may be so with you! May your progress, though slow perhaps, be genuine! And if you would have it so, use the means which I have already pointed out — such as public prayer, the hearing of the Gospel, partaking of the Lord's Supper, private reading of the Scriptures, secret prayer, intercourse with the Lord's people.

Ah, well is it if you are thus getting on, advancing, making progress! Well is it if you are gaining fresh victories over sin; if clearer light is breaking in upon you; if you are getting nearer to God, knowing Him better, and loving Him more; if you are feeling the ground firmer under you; and are fearing death less, and are desiring heaven more!

We must aim high, if we would win heaven. We must not be content to say, "I will live as others live." Try to live as the Word of God directs you. Try to live as St. Paul lived, and St. Peter, and St. John, and others, who are now with God. Above all, try to live as Jesus lived when He was among us. Holiness is happiness; and sure I am that he who lives the holiest life lives the happiest life. Seek to be a rejoicing, happy Christian, living above the world, and daily pressing towards the mark for the prize of your high calling in Christ.

Go on, my dear fellow-Christian; and may God help you on your way! He promises to do so: "I will be (he says) as the dew unto Israel; he shall grow up as the lily, and cast forth his roots as Lebanon." (Hos. xiv. 5.) "They that wait upon the Lord shall renew their strength; they shall mount up with wings as eagles; they shall run and not be weary." Is. xl. 31.

But possibly some one who has been reading these pages, may have a little misgiving as to his own state. His conscience, all the while, may have been whispering, "Alas, it is not so with me! So far from getting on, I am falling back. There was a time when I felt much more than I now feel. My heart has grown cold. I have not the same delight in prayer that I once had. My Bible is not so welcome to me."

A relapse! What state can be more sad? To have known God—to have loved Him—to have fled to Christ—to have given Him your heart—and then to have gone from Him, and to have allowed the world to steal in again—this is indeed a melancholy state of things! And oh, if such be *your* state, listen to a friendly counsellor. God has a word for you, it may be, on this very page which you are reading. He would call you back, and stop you in your downward course.

My dear reader, if you are a backslider; if you have gone aside, though it be only a step or two; if you have fallen back, though it may be only a little way perhaps; I beseech you to stop. Thank God, it is not too late for you to return. Take up your neglected Bible again. Fall humbly on your knees, and ask God to pour out upon you afresh the spirit of prayer. Give yourself to Him anew. Say to Him, " Lord, revive thy work in my soul. Restore unto me the joy of thy salvation."

> " Return, O holy dove, return,
> Sweet messenger of rest ;
> I hate the sins that made Thee mourn,
> And drove Thee from my breast."

But it may not be quite so bad with you as this. You may not have entirely relapsed. You may be in a *stagnant* state. The stream may not be actually dried up, though it does not flow on. There are some in the world, of whom it would be wrong to say that they are not God's children ; for many marks shew them to be His. They have deep convictions of conscience, and strong feelings of their guilt and misery; they have willingly given up many worldly advantages for Christ; and it is their desire to live " unblameable and unreprovable in his sight." But there they stand, motionless, as it were. They have got thus far, but they make no advance. They have been " brought up out of the horrible pit," in which they were once sunk; but there they are content to be, at the pit's mouth, as it were, instead of rising up, and pressing onwards towards heaven. They are much as they were weeks and months back. Their troubles and their temptations are just the same as they were then. They have got over none of their difficulties. They do not ripen. They do not " mount up with wings as eagles." They do not *run*, but *crawl*, towards heaven.

Now, where this is the case, there must be something wrong. There must be some secret hidden sin allowed, or some known duty left undone. The plant must have some canker at the root, or it would grow. There is a fulness of blessing in Christ: but perhaps a lack of prayer for it on your part. You "have not, because you ask not." Can you expect the fire to burn brightly, if you do not feed it? Can you expect the wheels to go round, if you let no oil into them? Can you expect the vessel to move onward in its course, if its sails are not spread to catch the wind? You will do well to examine yourself, and find out what is wanting in you. And then set out, as it were, *afresh*. Repent, as if you had never repented before. Go to Christ for a new grant of pardon; and begin today to live an earnest and devoted life.

But I would hope that neither of these states is yours; that you are neither going back, nor standing still; but that you feel yourself to be getting on. Your conscience tells you that you are getting on by little and little. Still *you must be watchful*. He that feels strong today may be weak tomorrow. Remember, your strength does not lie in yourself, but in the Lord. You stand, only so long as He supports you. You advance, only so far as He helps you on. Neither does God give you a stock of grace; but just enough for your present wants. Let your daily prayer then be,

"Hold thou me up, and I shall be safe," (Ps. cxix. 117.) And as you run your race, be ever "looking unto Jesus, the Author and Finisher of your faith." Heb. xii. 2.

> Think what Spirit dwells within thee;
>   Think what Father's smiles are thine;
> Think that Jesus died to win thee—
>   Child of heaven, canst thou repine?
>
> Haste thee on from grace to glory,
>   Armed by faith, and winged with prayer;
> Heaven's eternal day before thee,
>   God's own hand shall guide thee there.
>
> Soon shall close thy earthly mission,
>   Soon shall pass thy pilgrim days:
> Hope shall change to glad fruition,
>   Faith to sight, and prayer to praise.

Christian, let your motto be — "Forward, Onward, Heavenward!" Set yourself daily to some *heart*-work. Try and overcome some sin. Be ever putting on some Christian grace. Be ever getting some new thoughts of Christ. Be constantly seeking to pick out some pearl from God's word. Deny yourself in some fresh particular. Get some fresh glimpse of God and of heaven. "Grow in grace, and in the knowledge of our Lord and Saviour Jesus

Christ." Let your path be as the sun—that bright and "shining light, which *shineth more and more* unto the perfect day."

SYMPTOMS OF A DECLINING STATE.
(Gathered chiefly from "The Pocket Prayer-book.")

1. When you grow bolder with sin, or with temptations to sin, than you were in your more watchful state — then be sure something is wrong.

2. When you make a small matter of those sins and infirmities, which once seemed grievous to you, and almost intolerable.

3. When you settle down to a course of religion, that gives you but little labour, and leave out the hard and costly part.

4. When your God and Saviour grows a little strange to you; and your religion consists in conversing with *men and their books,* and not with *God and His book.*

5. When you delight more in hearing and talking, than in secret prayer and the word.

6. When you use the means of grace more as a matter of duty, than as food in which your soul delights.

7. When you regard too much the eye of man, and too little the eye of God.

8. When you grow hot and eager about some disputed point, or in forwarding the interests of some party of Christians, more than about those matters which concern the great cause of Christ.

9. When you grow harsh and bitter towards those who differ from you, instead of feeling tenderly towards all who love Christ.

10. When you make light of preparing for the Lord's Day, and the Lord's Table, and think more of outward ordinances than you do of heart-work.

11. When the hopes of heaven and the love of God cannot interest you; but you are thirsting after some worldly enjoyment, and grow eager for it. When the world grows sweeter to you, and death and eternity are distasteful subjects.

ALL THESE ARE SURE SIGNS OF A DECLINING STATE.

CHAPTER XVI.

THE DISCIPLINE OF AFFLICTION.

You have doubtless visited a Stonemason's workshop. There you have seen stones of every shape—some rough and coarse, and some smooth and even. And you have observed also a number of tools—some sharp for cutting the stone, and some for grinding and smoothing it. Now, the Church on earth is God's workroom. Here He prepares the stones for his spiritual temple above. And we usually find, that on those which He specially values, and means to fit for some great purpose, He employs his sharpest tools.

Thou art a child of God—then marvel not if thou art afflicted. For is it not written, "Whom the Lord loveth he chasteneth, and scourgeth every son whom he receiveth. If ye endure chastening, God dealeth with you as with sons; for what son is he whom the father chasteneth not?" (Heb. xii. 6, 7.) And Jesus himself says, "As many as I love, I rebuke and chasten." (Rev. iii. 19.) The Gardener cuts and prunes his fruit-trees. Why? but that they may be the more vigorous and healthy. And so does the heavenly Husbandman deal with the living branches of his vine; "Every branch *that beareth fruit*, he purgeth it, that it may bring forth *more fruit*." (John xv. 2.) The Shepherd, as he watches over his sheep, sometimes employs a dog to gather them. They are straying perhaps on the mountains, and he would thus call them home. The dog seems for a while to be only scaring and scattering the sheep; but in the end he brings them together, close to his master's side. So does the Lord send affliction and trial after us. He makes us suffer for a while. But it is for our profit; and it matters little, if we are thereby brought into the fold for safety.

It may be, you have prayed that God would make you all that He would have you to be; that He would cast you in his own mould, and conform you to his blessed image. He hears your prayer, and answers it—but how? Not perhaps in the way you would wish. But He sends you some trial, some chastisement. He lays you down upon a sick-bed; or He removes some dear one from you; or He overthrows some of your plans; or He sends you persecution. In short, He brings you under His chastening rod; and thus, though He seems to be punishing you, He is really blessing you.

Ah! we sometimes feel it hard, at the time, to be thus dealt with. The cross is painful and burdensome when it comes, and we flinch beneath it. We looked, it may be, for a very different answer to our prayer. We expected that the Lord would gently pour His grace into our souls. But instead of this, He laid His heavy hand upon us. Our feeling is just that which is so beautifully described by the Christian poet:—

> "I asked the Lord that I might grow
> In faith, and love, and every grace;
> Might more of his salvation know,
> And seek more earnestly his face.

> "I hoped that, in some favoured hour,
> At once He'd answer my request;
> And by his love's constraining power,
> Subdue my sins, and give me rest.

… THE DISCIPLINE OF AFFLICTION.

"Instead of this, He made me feel
  The hidden evils of my heart;
And let the angry powers of hell
  Assault my soul in every part.

"'Lord, why is this?' I trembling cried;
  'Wilt thou pursue thy worm to death?'
''Tis in this way,' the Lord replied,
  'I answer prayer for grace and faith.

"'These inward trials I employ,
  From self and pride to set thee free,
And break thy schemes of earthly joy,
  That thou may'st seek thy all in Me.'"

It is in the school of affliction that the Christian learns his best and holiest lessons. Thus it is he is made meet for heaven. His sufferings wean him from the world, and draw him closer to his Saviour. He is prepared for the crown of glory by wearing for a while the crown of thorns. In the silent hours of sorrow he becomes better acquainted with his own heart, and learns to know and to love Christ more. He is here taught a lesson of thankfulness; for never do we know the full value of a blessing until it is gone. Health, Children, Friends,—we must lose them before we know the preciousness they contain. He learns submission to his Father's will. He learns humility: and feels the blessedness of prayer. "In this path (says Winslow) he learns his own nothingness. And what a lesson is this to acquire! Other discipline may mortify, but not humble the pride of his heart—it may wound, but not crucify it. Affliction, sanctified by the Spirit of God, lays the soul in the dust, and gives it low thoughts of itself. Gifts, attainments, successful labours, the applause of men—all conspire to bring about the ruin of a child of God; and but for the prompt, and often severe, discipline of an ever-watchful and ever-faithful God, would accomplish his ruin. But the affliction comes —the needed cross—the required medicine. And in this way are brought out 'the peaceable fruits of righteousness.' It is the fire of affliction that searches and purifies the heart. It is here that the tin and tinsel are consumed. It is here the dross is separated from the true ore; and the gold is brought forth, reflecting back the image of Him, who, like the refiner, watches with tenderness and faithfulness the process of trial through which the precious metal is passing."

It is submission that God specially desires to work in us by affliction—the complete surrender of the will to Him in all things. "I speak not of this as an attainment in holiness soon or easily gained—far from it. In many it is the work of years—in all, of painful discipline. It is not on the high mount of joy, but in the low valley of humiliation, that this precious and holy surrender is to be learnt. It is not on the summer day, when all things smile and wear a sunny aspect—*then* it were easy to say, 'Thy will be done'—but when a cloudy and wintry sky looks down upon thee; when the chill blast of adversity blows; when health fails; when friends die; when wealth departs; when the heart's fondest endearments are yielded; when the *Isaac* is called for; when the world turns its back; when all is gone, and thou art brought like a tree in the desert, over which the tempest has swept, stripping it of every branch; when thou art brought so low, that it would seem to thee that lower thou couldst not be—*then* to look up, and exclaim, 'My Father, thy will be done!' Oh, this is holiness, this is happiness indeed."

"It may be, God, thy God and Father, is dealing thus with thee now. Has He taken away health? Have riches made to themselves wings? Does the world frown? Ah, little dost thou think how God is now about to unfold to thee the depths of his love, and to cause thy will sweetly and entirely to flow into His. Earnestly pray for it. Diligently seek it."

Do not be over anxious to have your affliction removed, but to have it made a blessing to you. Beware how you seek to push it from you, and escape from it, before the Lord's merciful purpose has been gained. An old writer, comparing affliction to a *prison*, observes that when God places us in it, we must not try to escape by breaking open the door. "Rather should we look patiently through the bars of the window; and when we see Him passing along, cry, 'Bring my soul out of prison, that I may praise thy name.'" Psalm cxlii. 7.

Perhaps this Book may be in the hands of some one who has long been a prisoner to a sick bed. And sometimes perhaps the feeling comes across you, "Oh that I could be more useful! I see other Christians actively employed in their Master's service; and here I lie still and useless." No, dear Reader, think not so. There is a work for you to do in your sick chamber—a work *as great* in God's eyes as that of the most busy labourer in His employment. Your work is " to sit still "—to glorify your Father by your patient, humble, cheerful resignation to His will, and by lying passive in His hands. The little quiet stream that trickles down the hill-side, almost unseen and unnoticed, is doing the work allotted to it, just as much as the mighty ocean which carries hundreds of ships on its restless bosom.

Job says, " When He hath tried me, I shall come forth as gold." (Job xxiii. 10.) And how many of God's children are the better, the holier, and the happier, for their affliction! We know that some flowers must be bruised, before they send out their full sweetness. And some Christians have need of trial, to make their graces appear; or their loving Father would gladly withhold it from them. Like the glowworm, they shine brightest in the darkest night.

And oh, how sweetly does affliction often-times form, and fashion, and mould, the Christian character! At the time, perhaps, we can hardly welcome it. We can scarcely persuade ourselves that it is the message of a beloved Friend. It "seemeth not to be joyous, but grievous." But "afterwards," when the first stunning blow is over, "it yieldeth the peaceable fruits of righteousness;" teaching us to know more of God than we ever knew before, bending our will to His, and conforming us gradually to His image. Oh, who can tell the blessing of affliction, when sanctified to us by the Spirit of God?

Are *you* one of God's afflicted servants? Is sickness your portion? Or do you meet with contempt and opposition? Or have some of your fondest hopes been disappointed? Know that your trial, *be it what it may*, is good for you. It is your Father's sending. Pray that it may be blessed to your soul. Pray that you may not only have a spirit of *resignation*, but also of *thankfulness*. Even a worldly man may be resigned, because he may feel that it is useless to resist God. But it is grace alone that can enable us to welcome affliction, because it is our Father's will. It is grace alone that can enable us to say with St. Paul, "I am *exceeding joyful* in all our tribulation." 2 Cor. vii. 4.

If your sufferings of mind or body are great, think of the "Man of sorrows:" His were greater. Bear them patiently and cheerfully for His sake. Say with Him, "The cup which my Father hath given me, shall I not drink it?" (John xviii. 11.) Think, too, how little is the weight of your sorrows, when compared with the "eternal weight of glory" which is before you. When present suffering seems to pull down the balance, and cause the scale which is nearest to you to droop heavily, place future bliss and glory in the opposite scale; and that will soon make the balance more than even. Remember, too, you have but a little while to bear your sorrows. A few more rough waves, and then you will be at rest. Another storm or two to ride out, and then you will reach "the haven where you would be." Meekly bear your cross now, and soon you shall wear the crown. If you are willing to "suffer with Christ" here, you shall reign with Him hereafter; you shall be with Him in that blissful world, where "sorrow and sighing shall flee away."

> "Lord, wave again thy chastening rod,
>   Till every idol-throne
> Crumble to dust; and thou, O God,
>   Reign in our hearts alone."

CHAPTER XVII.

USEFULNESS.

It is a glorious thing for the Christian that he has found acceptance in Christ, and that he enjoys peace within. But *something more* is needed. It is not enough for him to have his own salvation assured to him. He must not stop here. There are other important concerns which should interest him. "For what purpose was I sent into the world?" "How can I be useful in it?"—these are inquiries, which every earnest-hearted servant of Christ will be disposed to make.

Whatever our calling in life may be, we may glorify God, and be useful to others. Great things are sometimes accomplished by very feeble instruments. You have probably seen a little Silk-worm. It is a plain, common-looking insect. There is nothing remarkable in its appearance. But it feeds on the mulberry tree, digests its leaves, and spins from them a delicate silken ball. And this has given rise to a beautiful Persian saying,—" By patience and perseverance the mulberry leaf becomes satin."

Yes, great things may be accomplished by us all, if we have only a ready mind, and an earnest will. The Christian may be useful whilst he remains here—useful, whatever be his station in life.

But you may perhaps be ready to ask—*How can I be useful?* I will try and show you.

1. By *throwing yourself heartily into the ordinary duties of life.* You need not go out of your track to find ways of usefulness. God's work will be best done by a right performance of every-day duties.

You are a *Master* or a *Mistress*, I will suppose. Well then, take a real interest in the well-being of those about you. Try to make them better men and women for being under your roof. Do little acts of kindness towards them. And where you see that they are wrong, try and lead them into a better way. Let them feel that you are their friend, and not their superior only, and that you would gladly do them any service in your power.

Or you may be a *Servant*. Then do your work, whatever it be, conscientiously; not merely when your employer's eye is upon you, but when he is absent. Do it, not as unto man, but unto God. If there should be any dishonesty going on in the house, set your face against it; or if any quarrel should arise, try and be a peace-maker. You may be of great use among your fellow-servants. You may set the rest a good example, and so may lead many right. You may be a check upon one, an encourager of another, and you may show kindness to a third. And thus, in your humble position, you may be a blessing to the whole household.

Or again, you may be a *Farmer*, or a *Tradesperson*. In this station, many doors of usefulness will be daily opening themselves to you, if you look out for them. You may influence those about you for good. In your town, or in your parish, there is sure to be some opportunity for making yourself useful. Try and seize such opportunities. Be thoughtful of the wants of others, and ready to advise and assist them in their difficulties. And, at all events, let there be such uprightness and integrity in your whole conduct, as may plainly shew that there is within a principle of religion, guiding and directing you.

It is not our calling in life that will make us acceptable to God; neither is it by leaving our calling that we shall be enabled the better to serve Him. Judas was a minister and an apostle of Christ, but he was a castaway. Herod was a slave, though he sat upon a throne. On the other hand, who will say that the work of that carpenter's shop at Nazareth was not noble and kingly work indeed; for there was One there who could say amidst all his lowly toil, " Wist ye not that I must be about my Father's business?"

In short, in all the little every-day matters of life try and do as much good as you can. Be ever seeking to get a blessing yourself, and to be a blessing to others, wherever you are. Be a humble light-bearer in the midst of this dark world.

2. By *the holiness and consistency of your character.* Words often have but little effect, however well spoken; but a holy life is a most

powerful preacher. Let it be seen by those about you that religion has a firm hold of you; that you are living under its constraining power; and that, in all you do and say, it is the one mainspring that moves you.

We little know what a wholesome influence a holy walk may have upon others. The example and influence of a good man may tell upon the lives and conduct of hundreds.

For instance, a man may be going to do something wrong. He meets a friend in the street, whom he knows to be a religious person. Not a word may pass between them, and yet the very sight of his neighbour may lead the man to think of better things, and he may change his intention.

Have you not sometimes felt, that to be in the company of a holy servant of God only for a few minutes, though not one word may be spoken directly to you, has led you to go away thoughtful? There was something about his Christian bearing, which made you feel self-condemned. Thus, when we little know it, or intend it ourselves, we are continually influencing one another, either for good or for evil.

See, then, how useful you *may* be in your daily walk. You may be in a very humble station of life; you may have little or no learning; you may have no particular gift of speech; and yet you may be a blessing to those among whom you mix. Your light may shine, without your knowing it; your life may speak, when your tongue is silent. If you are living to Christ, you are a daily and hourly witness to the fact that there is a power in religion, which can make a man a blessing in this world of sin and sorrow.

One of our missionaries bears the following testimony to the good done by the consistent example of one of his Hindoo converts:— " By his uniform consistency, Peter (the name of the convert) had obtained a good report both of the brethren and of strangers. Hindoos and Mussulmans would often tell us, ' If all your Christians were like Peter, we would adopt your faith.' In his little transactions with the world, his word was as good as his bond. Any tradesman would trust his promise, in cases where he would have required a surety from one of his own creed." Oh, that this could be said of all who feel the power of religion in their hearts! But I must now mention another means by which you may be useful.

3. By *speaking for Christ*. I have shown what quiet, consistent influence may do. But we must not rest there. God has given us tongues, and we must speak for Him. And if the heart be full, it *will* find vent in words. You should try and persuade others to become the Lord's servants, whilst your own happy experience should show them, that His is a delightful service.

You know, perhaps, that one of your companions never reads his Bible. Speak to him a word in season on that subject. And be sure that it is *in season*—that is, when he is likely to receive advice kindly. Or, if there be another whom you never see in church, endeavour to lead him there by gentle persuasion. Avoid all harsh and reproachful language; or you will, in all probability, defeat your own purpose. Or, if from the lips of a third you occasionally hear an oath, do what you can to check him; speak to him at some time when he is alone, taking care that it shall be when he is calm, and not when he is excited. Or, it may be you are thrown in with some one who has evidently no serious thoughts about another world. Watch some favourable opportunity for directing his attention to those important matters which concern his soul.

But, on all occasions, *seize the right moment*, if possible, for putting in a word; for the Wise Man says, " A word spoken *in due season*, how good is it ! " And, again, he tells us that " a word *fitly spoken* is like apples of gold in pictures of silver." Prov. xv. 23; xxv. 11.

And always bear this in mind—that kind words go much farther than rough ones; that it is easier to *lead* a man than to *force* him. Never speak, then, as though you had *authority* to reprove or exhort; but bear yourself as towards a brother or a sister, with all humility and love.

4. Another means, by which you may be useful, is by *seeking some active employment in the Church*. Perhaps you can be of use as a Sunday-school Teacher, or as a Tract Distributor, or as a Visitor to the Sick, or as a Missionary Collector. Propose this to your clergyman; and he will, no doubt, find you work, and be glad to number you among his little labouring band. It is a happy thing to be thus employed; and you may well count it

but such as I have give I thee." (Acts iii. 6.) And you are thus pleasing God, and working for Him.

5. I will mention one more way by which we may be useful, namely by *Prayer*. Pray much for the work of religion in your Family, in your Parish, in the Church, and in the World at large. Your prayers should not be cramped. It is not merely for yourself that you should be concerned. Your interest should extend beyond your own little circle. You are a member of a great Christian Body, and you should be anxious that that Body may prosper. Your own parish, and your own minister, and your own congregation, of course, claim your first concern; but you should feel interested also in the welfare of other parishes, of other ministers, and of other congregations besides your own. And do not stop there. Do what you can to help forward Christ's kingdom in the world. And pray specially and constantly that God would pour out His Spirit, and bless the efforts of those who are labouring for Him.

Who can tell what blessings would come down upon any place or country, if earnest, untiring, believing prayer were daily offered in its behalf? "Prove me now herewith, saith the Lord of hosts, if I will not open you the windows of heaven, and pour you out a blessing, that there shall not be room enough to receive it." Mal. iii. 10.

Now, some, if not all, of these ways of usefulness are within your reach. You have talents committed to you : use them to God's glory. Each one of us has his own allotted post to fill in the Church, and in the World. And happy will it be for you if your little span here is thus usefully employed! "There is," says a Christian writer, "work for *all* of us. And there is a special work for *each*—a work which, if I do it not, must be left undone. No one of my fellows can do that particular work for me which I have come into the world to do. He may do a higher work—a greater work—but he cannot do *my* work for me. I must do it with these hands, or with these lips, which God has given me. I may do little, or I may do much ; *that* matters not: it must be *my own work*. The low grass tuft is not the branching elm, nor is it the fragrant rose. But it has a work to do in the arrangements but such as I have give I thee." (Acts iii. 6.) And you are thus pleasing God, and working for Him.

5. I will mention one more way by which we may be useful, namely by *Prayer*. Pray much for the work of religion in your Family, in your Parish, in the Church, and in the World at large. Your prayers should not be cramped. It is not merely for yourself that you should be concerned. Your interest should extend beyond your own little circle. You are a member of a great Christian Body, and you should be anxious that that Body may prosper. Your own parish, and your own minister, and your own congregation, of course, claim your first concern; but you should feel interested also in the welfare of other parishes, of other ministers, and of other congregations besides your own. And do not stop there. Do what you can to help forward Christ's kingdom in the world. And pray specially and constantly that God would pour out His Spirit, and bless the efforts of those who are labouring for Him.

Who can tell what blessings would come down upon any place or country, if earnest, untiring, believing prayer were daily offered in its behalf? "Prove me now herewith, saith the Lord of hosts, if I will not open you the windows of heaven, and pour you out a blessing, that there shall not be room enough to receive it." Mal. iii. 10.

Now, some, if not all, of these ways of usefulness are within your reach. You have talents committed to you: use them to God's glory. Each one of us has his own allotted post to fill in the Church, and in the World. And happy will it be for you if your little span here is thus usefully employed! "There is," says a Christian writer, "work for *all* of us. And there is a special work for *each*—a work which, if I do it not, must be left undone. No one of my fellows can do that particular work for me which I have come into the world to do. He may do a higher work—a greater work—but he cannot do *my* work for me. I must do it with these hands, or with these lips, which God has given me. I may do little, or I may do much; *that* matters not: it must be *my own work*. The low grass tuft is not the branching elm, nor is it the fragrant rose. But it has a work to do in the arrangements of God, which neither elm nor rose can undertake."

Another writer makes the following valuable observations:—"Every Christian will desire to do good in his day and generation. *All* can do something. There are two vast scales before us all, one for good, and one for evil; one for Christ, and one against Him. Our influence must go in one scale or the other. The least and lowest has one grain, at all events, in his hand. Let each see that he throws that grain into the right scale. Every Christian will desire to leave the world a better world than he found it—more godly, more enlightened, more happy. He will desire, if possible, to lessen the amount of evil, and to do his part in clearing some of it away. Let the selfish worldling reck little how the world goes on, and care nothing, if it only lasts his time. The true Christian is of another kind. I believe it behoves a true Christian to take an interest in everything which affects the religion of his Church and Country. The mouse in the fable climbed to the top of the box in which he was born, and wondered to see the world so large. I fear there are many Christians very like him they only look within, at their own little box."

There are two Christian sayings which I would recommend to your notice :—

"Live, whilst you live."

"Do what you can, whilst you can."

Dear reader, seek to live to some purpose. Work "while it is day;" for your day is but a very short one, and then cometh "the night, when no man can work." Let your humble prayer be, that the world may be somewhat the better, and not the worse, for your stay in it.

A Christian minister, whose years were drawing to a close, once said, "When I die, I shall have my greatest grief, and my greatest joy—my greatest grief, that I have done so little for Jesus; my greatest joy, that He has done so much for me."

The religion of many Christians has this fault in it—they are too much occupied with *self*. Their religion mainly consists in a doubting anxiety about their own spiritual safety. This continues week after week, and month after month; and all the while they are perhaps leaving undone some work which God has evidently appointed for them. Indeed, if they were only doing the work, the doubts which harass them would, in all probability, speedily disappear.

Who is it that suffers most from fears about his *bodily* condition? Who is it that is for ever complaining of pains and aches, and is alarmed at every little change in his pulse? Is it the labourer, whose time is well employed from morning till night? Is it the man of business, whose farm or merchandise keeps his hands and head constantly at work? No; it is generally the person who has no settled occupation, who has no fixed and definite work to perform.

And so is it with Christians: the most constantly and usefully employed are generally the healthiest and strongest Christians. It is those who think they have no work to do for God, and who do none, that are usually distressed with harassing doubts and fears as to their condition.

To such I would say, rouse yourselves to some active Christian duty. There is plenty of work to be done, and few ready to do it. Oh! it is a happy thing to labour for God; to take some little share in the great work, which He is employing His servants to do!

It is true, what we can do is at best but very little. But if that little is done heartily for the Lord, He will graciously own it. He will, in mercy, pardon what is amiss, and accept our willing service. Happy will it be for us, if we shall hereafter be able to say—not as our blessed Lord said, "I have glorified thee on the earth;" for who among us can hope to say that?—but, " Lord, it has been *my humble aim* to glorify thee on the earth, and to finish the work which thou gavest me to do." John xvii. 4.

CHAPTER XVIII.

HAPPINESS.

The Christian's life is a happy one. He has his trials, as well as other men. But then his very sorrow is lightened; nay, it even ceases to be sorrow, for it is "turned into joy." The darkest clouds that hover over him have "a silver lining." He often passes through the furnace, but there is One at hand to cheer and comfort him. "These words," said Jesus, "have I spoken unto you, that in me ye might have peace. In the world ye shall have tribulation: but be of good cheer; I have overcome the world." (John xvi. 33.) "Many," says the Psalmist, "are the afflictions of the righteous; but the Lord delivereth him out of them all." Psalm xxxiv. 19.

The Christian's happiness comes from God. He is the true Fountain of happiness; and there is no real happiness but that which flows from this Fountain. There may be riotous mirth, but that is not happiness; for may it not be said, that " even in laughter the heart is sorrowful, and the end of that mirth is heaviness?" (Prov. xiv. 13.) There may be short fits of joyous and excited feeling; but this does not make happiness, any more than the bright lightning which flashes across the midnight sky, and lights it up for a moment, turns night into day. Happiness, to deserve the name, must be something deep, calm, settled, and lasting; something which mere outward changes cannot shake or destroy; and such happiness comes only from God. See that yours is genuine; that it is no counterfeit coin; but that it has the stamp of heaven upon it. " We all know (says an able writer) the difference there is between a cloudy and a sunny day. The real heat may be the same; nay, the cloudy day may be the warmer of the two; yet to our feeling it may be quite the contrary. Now, in a man's spiritual condition we see much the same difference. Let God's face shine upon the soul; and it is cheered with the brightest sunshine. But let God veil His face, and cloud it over; and it feels chilled, and is discomforted. Thus it is written, ' Thou didst hide thy face, and I was troubled.' Do we not see in the world many a man disquieted and ill at ease in the very midst of earthly comforts, while his neighbour who lives in some sorry hovel may look always cheerful and contented? What is this difference owing to? To what cause must we trace the gloomy spirit of the one, and the blithe-hearted contentedness of the other, whose lot in the world's eye is so hard and wretched? The cause perhaps is simply this—the one is leading a Christian life: the other is living to the world —the one enjoys the light of God's countenance; from the other the Lord turns away His face, and leaves him in clouds and heaviness. Oh that you may know what it is to have the light of God's countenance lifted up upon you! Whenever that shines, it cheers and warms, it gilds and beautifies the lowest and meanest lot. Where that is wanting, happiness and peace are wanting also. For the good things of the world can no more make amends for it, than the blaze of lamps and torches can make amends for the absence of the sun."

What a mistaken notion does the world form of religion! It stamps the godly man as au unhappy man. Satan persuades people to believe that a religious life is a melancholy life; and thus he scares them from the ways of holiness. But the world has never had the veil lifted up. The world does not understand the Christian. Sure I am, that if religion does not make us happy, the fault is *in ourselves;* there must be something *in us* to prevent it. There must be some let or hindrance on our part. Either we must be naturally gloomy; or we have got hold of some mistaken views; or there is some sin indulged in, or some evil temper allowed. In short, *we* are to blame, and not our Lord. In Him is all fulness; but we oftentimes stop the stream of it into our own souls by impediments which we ourselves put in the way. The gospel of Christ not only bids us to rejoice, but also provides us with a source from which the truest happiness may flow, if we will but make it ours.

But mark this—*a little* religion will not give happiness. There are some persons who have just enough of it to make them *thoughtful*, but not enough to make them *happy*. They are dissatisfied with the world, and feel its emptiness, but they go no further. They know nothing of the joy and peace of Christ. But if you will give your whole heart to God, if you will live close to Him, obeying, loving, and serving Him, then I venture to promise that you will be happy. Earthly trials will pass gently over you; and, as for earthly joys, they will be nothing to you, when compared with that "peace which passeth all understanding," and which will fill your heart.

Is there not a happiness in feeling that you have in heaven a reconciled Father, who watches over you, and loves you—a Saviour, a Friend, full of tenderness and compassion, who ever liveth to make intercession for you; who knows all your wants, and has a balm for every wound? Is there not a peace in the consciousness that you are forgiven and accepted of God; and that, fare as you may here, there is before you a Home of peace, where you shall dwell for ever?

"Spiritual joy (says Archbishop Leighton) far exceeds the report that any one can give of it. It is 'joy unspeakable.' And when a man comes to know it in his own breast, he will say of it, as the Queen of Sheba said of Solomon's wisdom, 'The half was not told me.' (1 Kings x. 7.) Religion calls us away indeed from carnal enjoyments; but it is to give us those which are pure and lasting. It seems to say to us, 'Drink no longer of the puddle; here are crystal streams from a living fountain.'"

It is not, however, always those who *speak* most of this joy that *have* most of it. The deepest waters usually run the stillest: and sometimes the heart is too full to tell out all its contents. "The laughter of a fool," says Solomon, is "as the crackling of thorns under a pot." (Eccl. vii. 6.) There is a great blaze and noise, but it is soon over. But he who can say, " The righteousness of Christ is mine; the favour of God, and a bright hope of glory are, through God's grace, my blessed portion" —he has such a light within him, as can shine in the darkest dungeon; yea, even in the valley of the shadow of death itself.

Truly it is a blessed thing to be *a Christian ;* but still more blessed to be *a rejoicing Christian*. Now, this is within the reach of all of us. It is your duty and your privilege to seek for it. Try to be so, even when outward things are against you. Fair-weather Christianity (says one) is common enough; but the Christianity that will maintain its brightness in the dark and cloudy day of adversity is too frequently wanting. And yet what will so convince the unconverted of the reality of your profession, as showing that the evenness of your temper, the peacefulness of your mind, the happiness of your home, do not merely or mainly depend on the creature; but that in the midst of abounding disappointments and difficulties there can still be joy in the Lord? Open your Bible, and there you will read the command, "Rejoice evermore;" "Rejoice in the Lord always; and again I say, Rejoice." 1 Thess. v. 16; Phil. iv. 4.

Seek to be happy *for your own sake.* What a bright colouring it will give to your whole life! Seek to be happy *for the sake of others.* Will it not act as a charm to draw them also into the path, which you have found so sweet? Seek to be happy *for your Saviour's sake.* For thus you will be honouring Him, and bringing glory to His cause.

The religion of Christ is no gloomy thing. It gives a brightness and a reality to all our earthly ties. As Parents, it makes us anxious to further the happiness of our children. As Masters, it stirs up within us a desire to promote the comfort and well-being of those who are under our care. As Brothers and Sisters, it teaches us to give up our own wills, and to endeavour to please, and assist, and comfort each other.

Would you be a happy Christian? Then live much on Christ. Regard Him as your Friend —your unseen, but ever-living, ever-present Friend. Let Him be your refuge in every difficulty, your hope under every sorrow, your portion in the midst of an empty world. Here is the only true home for the believing heart. Nothing less will satisfy and fill it. You are weak, very weak; but here is your strength. Even the feeble ivy is strong, and able to climb high, when it clings to the sturdy tree; and so will you be, if you lay hold of Him who is able to bear you up. "In the Lord have I righteousness and strength." Live in humble, admiring, self-forgetting, fellowship with Him.

Would you be a happy Christian? Then be a *holy* Christian. Is there a child in any family who seems to be happier than the rest? It is the one who is ever desiring to obey his parents, and delighting to please them. And so the child of God, who loves his heavenly Father, and walks in His holy ways, enjoys a happiness which the world could never give him. Holiness is the groundwork of the

Christian's happiness: "If our heart condemn us not, then have we confidence towards God." (1 John iii. 21.) It has been well said, that happiness is a plant that grows nowhere but in holy ground. It is God's will that happiness and holiness should go together. And what is it that makes the bliss of heaven? Is it not that sin shall be for ever banished, and we shall dwell in the presence of a holy God?

Again, would you be a happy Christian? Then be a *thankful* Christian. Few think enough of their mercies. We are apt to take them too much as a matter of course. We ask eagerly for blessings; but when they come, we feel little or no thankfulness. We receive the gifts, but forget to render thanks to the almighty Giver. I am disposed to think that but few, in their devotions, spend time enough in praise. It is true, God is not the richer nor the happier for our thanks. He is not a whit the more blessed for our blessing Him. No, it is *we* who are the gainers by it. It is *we* who are made happy by it. God is graciously pleased to accept our thanks; and the very offering of them contributes to our happiness. Are we not told that "it becometh well the just to be thankful"? Psalm xxxiii. 1.

Only make the trial, and endeavour to live more thankfully. You will, I am sure, find that the very effort to be thankful will be good for you. "*In everything* give thanks, for this is the will of God in Christ Jesus concerning you." (1 Thess. v. 18.) "Thankfulness (says a Christian writer) is a kindly way of petitioning God. Just as vapours drawn up from the earth return to it in showers again, so praise for old mercies brings down large supplies of new."

When St. Paul was journeying towards Rome as a prisoner, we are told that, meeting with some brethren whose sympathy and affection refreshed him, he "thanked God, and took courage." And so may it be—so should it be—always with us. We should be full of thankfulness and hope. This will cheer us on our way; it will make our course bright, and enable us to pass lightly over the trials of this weary world.

Oh then for a heart to praise the Lord! Oh for a cheerful, happy, willing obedience! Oh that we may be enabled to rejoice, not only when things go smoothly with us, but also when the waves of life are ruffled! May we have the same trusting spirit as the prophet had, when he declared, "Although the fig-tree shall not blossom, neither shall fruit be in the vines; the labour of the olive shall fail, and the fields shall yield no meat; the flock shall be cut off from the fold, and there shall be no herd in the stall (that is, though all the streams of earthly blessing be dried up), yet I will rejoice in the Lord; I will joy in the God of my salvation." Hab. iii. 17, 18.

Truly the Christian may be happy—very happy. His happiness, however, will still be imperfect here. It is a happiness intermixed with trials. But there is a world to come—a promised world of peace for the people of God—a world, though unseen, yet real. In that world there will be no sorrowful ones—no tears to bedew the cheeks—no wrinkles along the brow. In that world dwells our Lord; and "in his presence is fulness of joy; at his right hand there are pleasures for evermore." Psalm xvi. 11.

Think not that our work there will be a work of idleness. No, it will be one of ceaseless activity. "His servants shall serve Him." We know not what our exact service will be in that happy world. But doubtless there is a work to be carried on in the Church above, as well as in the Church on earth. We must not suppose that a man's activity and usefulness will be at an end when he leaves the world. If Christ has employment for his servants here, He has a *higher* employment for them there—a holier, happier, more satisfying labour. Some heavenly work will occupy us day and night. Is God's service a delight to us *now?* Such will it be *then,* only in a thousandfold greater degree. Spiritual communion, praise, waiting upon God, bending our will to his, doing his pleasure ; hands, heart, voices; all engaged in his service—this will be our happiness in heaven—this will be our joyful occupation throughout eternity.

Our companions too will be holy—a spotless flock—"washed in the blood of the Lamb," and "clothed in white robes." And we ourselves shall then be perfectly holy also. We shall be sinless, and therefore sorrowless; full of love, full of light, knowing all things. Here, on this sea of life, the Christian is tossed, and well nigh shattered by many a rough storm; but in that quiet haven of rest, not a wave shall reach him. He will be safe in the presence of his Lord.

Go on then, my dear Christian friend; " ask the way to Zion with your face thitherward." Let nothing turn you from *the pathway of safety*. A few more trials, and then shall come the recompense. A little more bearing of the cross, and then you shall wear the crown. Another hard struggle or two, and then will come the victory! Hear the words of Him, who is seated at his Father's right-hand, "TO HIM THAT OVERCOMETH WILL I GRANT TO SIT WITH ME IN MY THRONE, EVEN AS I OVERCAME, AND AM SET DOWN WITH MY FATHER IN HIS THRONE." Rev. iii. 21.

LONDON: WILLIAM MACINTOSH, 24, PATERNOSTER-ROW.

www.ingramcontent.com/pod-product-compliance
Lightning Source LLC
Chambersburg PA
CBHW022117230426
43672CB00008B/1419